American Events

THE TRAIL OF TEARS

David K. Fremon

New Discovery Books
New York

Maxwell Macmillan Canada
Toronto

Maxwell Macmillan International
New York   Oxford   Singapore   Sydney

Book design: Deborah Fillion
Cover photo courtesy of Woolaroc Museum, Bartlesville, Oklahoma.

New Discovery Books
Macmillan Publishing Company
866 Third Avenue
New York, NY 10022

Maxwell Macmillan Canada, Inc.
1200 Eglinton Avenue East
Suite 200
Don Mills, Ontario M3C 3N1

Macmillan Publishing Company is part of the Maxwell Communication
Group of Companies.

First Edition

Printed in the United States of America

10 9 8 7 6 5 4 3 2 1

Library of Congress Catologing-in-Publication Data

Fremon, David K.
    The trail of tears / by David K. Fremon. — 1st ed.
        p. cm. (American events)
    Includes bibliographical references (p.   ) and index.
    ISBN 0-02-735745-7
    1. Cherokee Removal, 1838—Juvenile literature. 2. Cherokee Indians—
History—Juvenile literature. [1. Cherokee Removal, 1838. 2. Cherokee
Indians—History.   3. Indians of North America—Southern States—History.]
I. Title. II. Series.
E99.C5F73 1994
973'.04975—dc20   93-29723
    Summary: A history of the events leading up to the removal of the
Cherokee Nation from lands east of the Mississippi to the west in order
to make more room for white farmers.

Dedicated to Kent Joseph Fremon

and his Cherokee ancestors

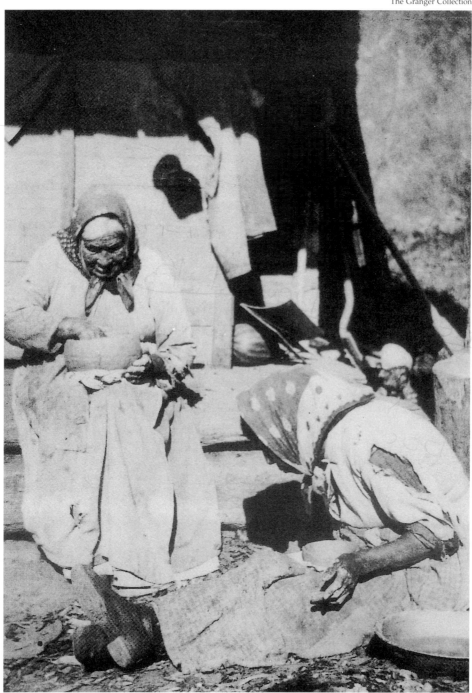

A Cherokee woman and her daughter make clay pots on a reservation.

CONTENTS

Native Americans who resisted forced removal from their lands were often treated brutally by soldiers.

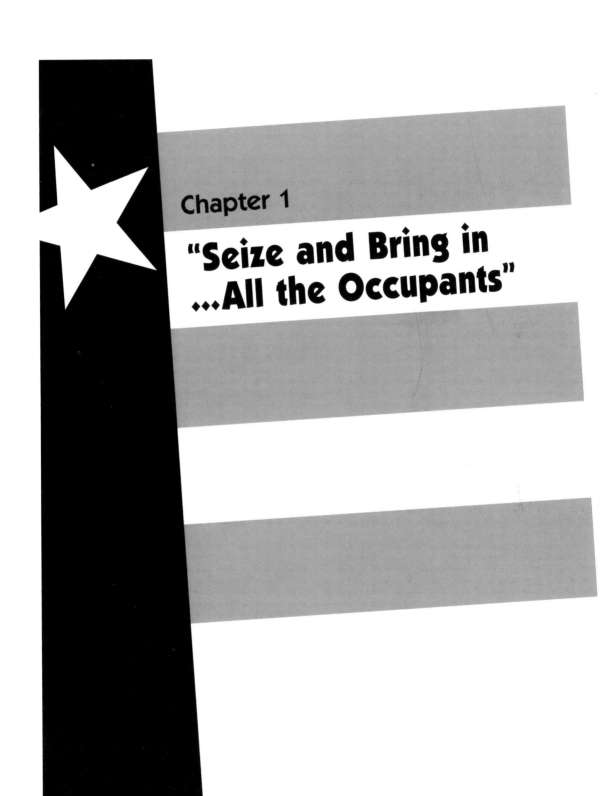

Chapter 1

"Seize and Bring in ...All the Occupants"

They came as suddenly as a tornado and caused as much damage. U.S. soldiers roused the Cherokees from their peaceful pursuits in the summer of 1838 and ordered them to start marching. Families at dinner were interrupted by troops knocking at their doors, the troops' bayonets gleaming in the setting sun. Farmers were pulled from their fields, women from their spinning wheels, children from their play, old people living alone from their simple homes in the hills.

These scenes repeated themselves throughout the vast Cherokee Nation. General Winfield Scott ordered the troops to search out "every small cabin hidden away in the coves or by the sides of mountain streams, to seize and bring in as prisoners all the occupants."[1]

Some soldiers showed a little kindness. One group allowed a family to pray before leading them from their home. Another squad gave a woman a few minutes to feed her chickens one last time. But others were cruel. Families away on visits were not allowed to return home. One group captured a hunter bringing home a deer. He was hauled into a detention camp while the soldiers ate his venison. Two children saw the advancing troops and ran into the woods. Their mother begged the soldiers to wait until she could find them, but they refused.[2]

Rebecca Neugin was only three years old when the soldiers came. Decades later, she remembered the scene vividly:

> When the soldiers came to my house my father wanted to fight, but my mother told him that the soldiers would kill him if he did, and he surrendered without a fight. They drove us out of our house to join other prisoners in a stockade. After they took us away, my mother begged them to let her go back and get some bedding. So they let her go back and she brought what bedding and a few cooking utensils she could carry and we left behind all our other household possessions.[3]

The Cherokees, once warlike but now quiet, were being driven from their land. The troops rounded up almost 17,000 of them and herded them into military stockades. Later they marched them to the distant Oklahoma territory—a new "homeland" promised them by a treaty that most tribe members opposed.

Before the exploitation of their lands by greedy settlers, the Cherokees lived simply and freely.

Chapter 2

"The Sole and Exclusive Masters of This Territory"

Cherokee legend says that the tribe sprang from the clouds and the earth. As late as 1830, testifying before the United States Supreme Court, Cherokees claimed they "derived their title from the Great Spirit (Asga-Ya-Galun-lati), who is father of the human family and to whom the whole earth belongs. Composing the Cherokee Nation, they and their ancestors are the sole and exclusive masters of this territory, governed by their own laws, usages, and customs."[1]

The land they claimed was hilly and fertile, filled with bountiful game and rushing streams, with tall forests and beautiful sunsets. Few who visited this land questioned the Cherokees' love for it.

One such visitor was Spanish conquistador Hernando de Soto. He and his troops encountered a village of people known as the Tsalagi in 1540. The Spaniards pronounced the name "Chalague"; years later the English would call the tribe "Cherokee."

The Cherokee occupied about 43,000 square miles (111,370 square kilometers) of territory, from the Ohio River on the north to the Chattahoochie River on the south and from the Blue Ridge Mountains on the east to the Mississippi River on the west. The land covered all or part of the present-day states of Kentucky, Tennessee, Alabama, Georgia, South Carolina, North Carolina, Virginia, and West Virginia. With 25,000 people, the Cherokee were the largest tribe in North America.

Lacrosse was a favorite sport of the Cherokee people, who once roamed over an area that now makes up several states in the southeast.

They also might have been the most violent. Englishman William Fyffe commented: "War is their principal study....Those houses on which there's the greatest number of scalps are the most honored."[2]

All Cherokee towns had a central Town House, where meetings took place. These houses had eight sides, one for each of the great clans. There were seven human clans. Bears were originally the eighth clan. According to Cherokee legend, they could talk like anyone else but wisely chose to keep silent.[3]

Cherokees played a ball game similar to lacrosse. Each town had a team, and games between rival towns were the highlight of festivals. Teams

Foreign traders won the trust of the American Indians by giving them small gifts.

had up to 50 players on a side, and a player might be kicked, punched, or even killed without a penalty.[4]

In the 1600s and early 1700s English traders brought the Cherokees cloth, axes, and trinkets. But the English gift the Indians relished most was guns. With these new weapons, the Cherokees routed their ancient enemies, the Tuscaroras. Then they fought the Creeks, Shawnees, and other rival tribes.

In 1730, the Cherokees welcomed an English trader named Alexander Cumming. He invited Chief Attakullakulla ("Little Carpenter") and six other tribal leaders to visit his homeland. The Cherokees became the rage of England. They were wined and dined everywhere. Their hosts invited them to the theater and gave them the finest clothes. The English considered the Cherokees so exotic that one innkeeper charged Londoners admission to watch them eat.[5]

The British Empire got more than entertainment from their visitors. Attakullakulla and the other Cherokees signed a treaty. It promised that the English would be the Cherokees' exclusive trading partners, that the Cherokees would fight for England in wars against other European powers, and that any English citizen accused of wrongdoing in Cherokee lands could be tried in an English court.

Attakullakulla met with King George II and proclaimed: "We look upon the great King George as the Sun and as our father....For though we are red and you are white, yet our hands and hearts are joined together."[6] The English, in turn, promised friendship for "as long as the mountains and rivers shall last, or the sun shines."[7]

A few years later, in 1738, English traders accidentally introduced the smallpox virus into the American population. Half the Cherokee Nation perished. Some died of the disease itself; others took their own lives after viewing their disfigured faces. The disaster was not intentional, since the English had no desire to harm the Cherokees. They enjoyed a lively trade. Clay from Cherokee lands was the main ingredient in prized English pottery. More important, the Cherokee allies proved a bulwark of defense against England's main enemy, the French.

England and France had been foes in Europe for centuries. By the mid-1700s, their animosity extended to a world war. England had established a string of colonies along North America's Atlantic Coast; the French loosely controlled the continent's interior. The North American conflict between these powers was known as the French and Indian Wars.

The French often tried to win the Cherokees' favor, yet Attakullakulla's promise to befriend the English was a sacred trust. Unlike most major Indian tribes, the Cherokees remained loyal to the English.

A young colonial army officer named George Washington praised the Cherokees' fighting skills, saying, "They will be of particular service—more than twice their number of white men." But he worried, "One false move…might turn them against us."[8]

Before the wars with the French were over, the English had nearly annihilated their supposed allies. It started with a misunderstanding in late 1759, when a group of Cherokees lost most of their provisions when a boat capsized in an icy river. They tried to borrow some horses from nearby Virginia settlers. The Virginians, thinking the Indians were horse thieves, shot 24 of them.

The colonial government apologized, but the apology was not accepted. Instead, the Cherokees slew two dozen whites in retribution. Killing led to more killing. Retaliation brought further retaliation. The Cherokees sued for peace in September 1760. This time, the English refused the peace offer.

Colonel James Grant led 2,000 troops in an invasion of Cherokee country. They burned 15 communities to the ground, laying to waste 1,500 acres of corn, beans, and peas. One of Grant's officers later wrote, "We proceeded…to burn the Indian cabins. Some of the men seemed to enjoy this cruel work, laughing heartily at the cruel flames.…When we came, according to orders, to cut down the fields of corn, I could scarcely refrain from tears."[9]

Once again, Attakullakulla sued for peace. This time the English destroyed the town of Echota. Only then did they grant peace to the Indians, who by this time were at the point of starvation.

The British won the French and Indian Wars and drove the French from North America. Afterward, they made laws prohibiting the inhabitants of their American colonies from moving west of the Appalachian Mountains. But the British had no way of stopping the settlers from crossing the mountains and claiming land of their own. The colonists no longer needed to worry about the French. Since more of them had learned how to trap their own furs, they had less use for the Cherokees.

In 1768, the Cherokees gave a small portion of little-used territory to the whites, hoping it would satisfy their hunger for land. But the white men wanted more. Seven years later, explorer Daniel Boone and land developer Richard Henderson bought much of modern Tennessee for ten million British pounds' worth of goods. A respected chief named Old Tassel rued, "If we had no lands, we should have fewer enemies."[10]

Attakullakulla's son, Tsinyu Gansini ("Dragging Canoe"), warned against the land deal. The tall, muscular warrior told his tribesmen:

> We hoped that white men would not be willing to travel beyond the mountains. Now that hope is gone. They have passed the mountains and have settled upon Cherokee land. When that is gained, the same encroaching spirit will lead them upon other lands of the Cherokees. New cessions will be asked. Finally the whole country, which the Cherokee have so long occupied, will be demanded, and the remnant of [the Cherokees], once so great and formidable, will be compelled to seek refuge in some distant wilderness. There they will be permitted to stay a short while, until they again behold the advancing banners of some greedy host. Not being able to point out any further retreat for the miserable Cherokees, the extinction of the whole race will be proclaimed.[11]

Tribal elders called Dragging Canoe a foolish hothead. In truth, he was amazingly prophetic. He and his followers left the main tribe and established a settlement near Chickamauga Creek in northern Georgia. From there they conducted a 20-year hit-and-run war against the whites. His guerrilla tactics led to a drive for revenge by American settlers.

On July 4, 1776, the 13 American colonies declared their independence from the British crown. To the British, this declaration meant war. North American tribes were left with a dilemma: which of these sides to back.

Members of other tribes came to the Cherokees in early 1776 and urged a united front against all whites. The Cherokees, however, saw colonial Americans, who were advancing into their territory, as more of a threat than the British. They picked the wrong enemy. Some Cherokees, along with whites disguised as Indians, attacked outlying settlements in the Carolinas. More than 5,000 frontiersmen retaliated by ravaging houses, livestock, fields, and orchards, scalping Cherokee men, and capturing Cherokee women and children. A devastated tribe sought peace in 1777, a peace that cost them five million acres of land on the Nation's northern and eastern borders.

In 1785, the government of the newly formed United States arranged its first treaty with the Cherokees. This treaty, signed in Hopewell, South Carolina, declared that the Cherokees were "under the favor and protection of the United States," although the Cherokees and other Native Americans were not considered American citizens. The treaty showed the government's inability to enforce its rulings. Settlers were ordered to leave Cherokee lands, but most ignored the order.

Many of the white settlers came to live in peace. Some even married Cherokee women. From these unions came some of the most illustrious names in Cherokee history. Englishman William Shorey married a Cherokee woman, and their daughter Ann married John McDonald, a soldier. Their grandson, John Ross, although only one-eighth Cherokee, would lead the tribe for half a century. Nathaniel Gist, a soldier under George Washington, never married the woman he met in the Cherokee Nation. But their son, Sequoyah, would revolutionize Cherokee life.

Not all whites were peaceful. A onetime American soldier named John Sevier led about 500 followers from North Carolina and proclaimed the District of Franklin on land that is now eastern Tennessee. This illegal action led to several years of bloodshed between Franklinites and Cherokees.

But the Cherokees had a powerful ally. George Washington, now president of the United States, wanted peace with Native Americans. He realized that a treaty not respected by whites would only lead to more violence. Washington ordered Sevier captured, then summoned Cherokee chiefs to Holston (now Knoxville), Tennessee, for a treaty in 1791.

The Holston treaty benefited both whites and Cherokees. It defined boundaries "for all time" between Cherokee and U.S. lands and promised "perpetual peace" between the two nations. It forbade Americans to hunt or fish on Cherokee lands without tribal permission. While Cherokees

The Granger Collection

One American leader who wanted peace with the Indians was George Washington, who had worked successfully with them during his years in the military.

charged with crimes against U.S. citizens would be tried in U.S. courts, Americans charged with crimes against Cherokees would be tried in Cherokee courts.

Most significantly, the treaty allowed the United States to give farm equipment and tools to the Cherokees. They were supplied with plows, spinning wheels, and other implements intended to transform them into farmers. This life-style change, in theory, would make the Cherokees more peaceful. And since farmers use less land than hunters, more land would be available to whites.

Dragging Canoe died in 1792, but his renegade followers continued their fruitless battles for two more years. The U.S. government, finally tiring of these guerrillas, sent troops against them to destroy their homes in 1794. The Americans demanded no new land from the resulting treaty. But they won the right to build forts and roads on Cherokee lands.

Doublehead, a follower of Dragging Canoe, tried to make his own peace with the white man. Unknown to the rest of the Cherokees, he arranged to sell some tribal land to Secretary of War Henry Knox, violating the most sacred Cherokee law. The law said any individual who sold land was to be punished by death. A young warrior called Ka-nin-da-da-geh ("The Ridge") shot Doublehead, then split his skull with a tomahawk. By carrying out the tribe's "blood law," he avenged Doublehead's treachery.

Peace now appeared to be at hand. But events in the United States affected the Cherokees. As the 18th century became the 19th century, the future would loom uncertain for the Cherokee Nation.

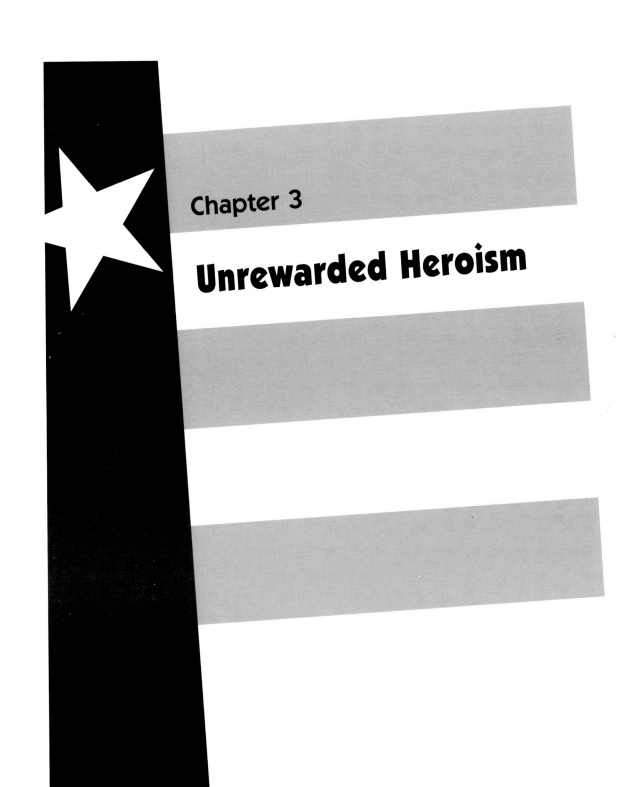

Chapter 3

Unrewarded Heroism

n 1791, Secretary of State Thomas Jefferson wrote:

> I am of the opinion...that the Indians have a right
> to the occupation of their lands, independent of the
> state within those chartered limits they happen to
> be: That until they cede them by treaty, no act of a
> state can give them right to such lands.[1]

Ten years later, Jefferson became president. As chief executive, he remained personally sympathetic to Native Americans, but he also realized that the United States of America was growing and that its citizens constantly wanted more land. By the time he became president, the white population west of the Appalachian Mountains was 700,000. Whites already outnumbered Indians eight to one.

In the nation's early years, individual states wielded more power than they do today. States could, and often did, ignore federal laws. Presidents often had to negotiate with those individual states. Jefferson made a deal with the state of Georgia. After the Revolutionary War, Georgia claimed lands extending to the Mississippi River. In 1802, the federal government bought Georgia's western lands for $1.25 million. Georgia also made the federal government promise to remove the Cherokees and other Indians from lands within the state of Georgia as early as "peaceably" possible. Both the federal and state governments appeared pleased with the compact. No one bothered to consult the Indians.

Two years later, Jefferson made another land deal. France's Emperor Napoleon Bonaparte needed funds for his costly European war. He sold the vast Louisiana Territory that France owned in North America to Jefferson for $15 million—two cents an acre.

Overnight, the United States doubled in size. The country now seemed to have more than enough land to satisfy the needs of its settlers. After all, Jefferson reasoned, it took four generations for colonists to move from the Atlantic Coast across the Appalachians. At that rate, he calculated, it would take 40 generations to settle land to the Pacific Coast.[2]

Farmers and adventurers refused to follow Jefferson's timetable. There was good, rich land in the South, and it was theirs for the taking. A generation earlier, these white settlers would have encountered the warlike Cherokee Nation. Instead, they found fenced farms, pens with cattle and pigs, and fine houses. The Cherokees had adapted well to the peaceful agrarian life-style; even their means of travel had changed greatly. In the late 1700s, not a single road existed in Cherokee lands. Ten years later, roads crisscrossed the Nation.

American dollars soon kept the Cherokees in check more effectively than guns or bayonets could. The American government opened a trading post on Cherokee lands. Indians brought in furs; whites traded silks and other luxury items. In time, the Cherokees became indebted to the trading post. If the Indians lacked money to pay their debts, the United States would always accept land.

One Tennessee resident seemed particularly interested in obtaining Cherokee land. By 1796, 27-year-old Andrew Jackson had become a wealthy lawyer. The new state of Tennessee made him its first member of the House of Representatives. Jackson constantly fought the Cherokees in Congress. He also used his influence to obtain much of their former lands from the federal government. Yet when Jackson mounted a campaign against the Creeks, a southern tribe, in 1812, he sought the Cherokees' help.

Tecumseh, son of a Shawnee chief, had earned a reputation among eastern tribes as a fearsome warrior. He visited the Cherokees in 1811, calling for an alliance among tribes and a return to the traditional Indian life. Cherokees, said Tecumseh, should renounce schools and books.

The Ridge and other leaders rejected the Tecumseh proposal. "We turned our ears," The Ridge later told President James Madison.[3] The Cherokees, after all, were not unhappy with the white man's culture.

The Creeks listened to Tecumseh's message, but they misunderstood it. Tecumseh favored an alliance of defense against further white advancement, not an attack upon American military units. But a Creek group known as the Red Sticks, because of their red war clubs, attacked Fort Mims in 1813, killing more than 400 whites at the Alabama River outpost. The slaughter proved to be costly.

The United States decided to retaliate against the Creeks, and the Cherokees had to choose sides. Not all Cherokees favored entering a fight on the side of the Americans. After all, American farmers kept encroaching on the lands of the Cherokee Nation. The Ridge argued for siding with General Jackson. The Americans had more people and military power than the Cherokees, he said. If the Cherokees had any hope of retaining their land, they needed the Americans' favor. One way to bring about that goodwill was by fighting against the Creeks. Other Cherokees, swayed by The Ridge's legendary oratory and his logic, agreed with him. More than 600 Cherokees followed The Ridge to fight for Jackson.

One warrior named Dasigeyayi ("Shoe Boots") claimed the power to repel enemy spears and stop enemy bullets in mid-air. He was so effective in battle that Jackson nearly believed his boasts.

Jackson commanded a number of future leaders in his Creek campaign. The Ridge took charge of the Cherokee troops. Jackson was so impressed by his military skills that he gave him the title Major Ridge. The chief cherished the title the rest of his life. A gimpy-legged soldier named Sequoyah served under Jackson. So did John Ross, as a scout.

Jackson's forces followed the Creeks to Horseshoe Bend of the Tallapoosa River in Alabama Territory. The Creeks' escape routes were

The Granger Collection

Tecumseh tries to stop the Red Sticks from massacring settlers at Fort Mims.

blocked, but they could hold off the enemy indefinitely. Hidden in the thick woods, they could fire upon the Cherokees and whites.

Across the Tallapoosa, Cherokees waited and watched. While some of them started firing to draw the Creeks' attention, others swam across the river. They took the Creeks' canoes and paddled them back across the river. Now the full Cherokee force recrossed the river.

The daring act took the Creeks by surprise. More than 600 Cherokees attacked the Creeks' rear flank. The battle was a disastrous defeat for the Creeks. Jackson's forces lost only 44 men, 18 of them Cherokees. Nearly 1,000 Creeks died.

Andrew Jackson finished the war with the reputation of a great Indian fighter. The Cherokees, however, were the real heroes of the struggle against the Creeks.

If Cherokees expected gratitude from the Americans for their heroism, they were mistaken. For many in the United States, the long-range goal was for all Indians east of the Mississippi River to yield their lands to the whites. This goal applied both to attacking tribes like the Creeks and cooperative ones like the Cherokees.

In the early months of the Creek War, Cherokee farmers supplied American soldiers with cattle, hogs, and corn, and with feed for the soldiers' horses. When the Cherokee troops returned home in 1814, many found that American soldiers had entered their land and stolen whatever they wanted. If anything, their allies had treated them worse than the Creeks had.

The worst offender was their commander, Andrew Jackson. Cherokees fought bravely in the Creek War. Afterward, the U.S. government took 23 million acres of Creek land as a settlement. But when the Cherokees demanded 4 million of those acres, Jackson called the claims "Cherokee intrigue."[4] In fact, Jackson demanded that 11 southern tribes—including the Cherokees—give up their Tennessee lands and move west.

Cherokee representative John Ross took the first of many trips to Washington, D.C., in 1816. He explained his tribe's problem to President James Madison. The short, portly president agreed with Ross that Jackson's demand for Cherokee land cession was unfair and unreasonable. Madison arranged a treaty in 1816 that assured the Cherokee of lands Jackson tried to take, plus gave them some of the former Creek land. The United States also paid $26,500 for permission to build more roads and maintain river traffic in the Nation.

Jackson was livid. He described the treaty as a "wanton, hasty, useless thing" and vowed to "undo it."[5] In 1816 he bribed a dozen chiefs to give up 3,500 square miles (9,065 square kilometers) of land south of the Tennessee River for $5,000 cash and $6,000 in annuities (subsequent annual

Andrew Jackson earned the reputation as being a fierce enemy of the Indians for his efforts to remove them forcibly from their lands.

payments). He later told Secretary of War John C. Calhoun, "It was found both well and polite to make a few presents to the chiefs and interpreters."[6]

James Monroe succeeded Madison as U.S. president in 1817. Unlike his predecessor, Monroe promoted treaties forcing the Cherokees to cede their land and stepped up efforts to get the Cherokee Nation to move West.

The Treaty of 1819 shrank the once-vast Cherokee Nation, costing

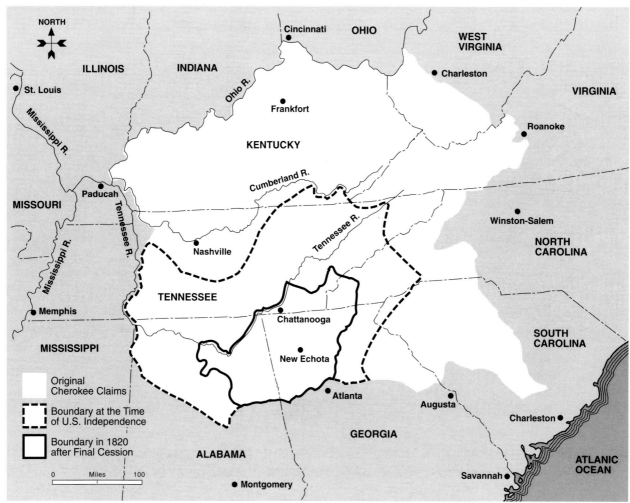

Shrinkage of the Cherokee Nation (East) at different stages in its history

the Cherokees about 10 million acres of land. Originally, the Cherokee Nation covered 43 million acres across eight present-day southern states. Now it covered only 10 million acres in Alabama, Tennessee, North Carolina, and Georgia.

Junaluska was one of the Cherokees who had fought with Jackson against the Creeks in the Battle of Horseshoe Bend. After the treaties, land cessions, and atrocities he said, "Oh my God, if I had known…I would have killed him that day at the Horseshoe!"[7]

Chapter 4

"Industrious and Intelligent People"

In any age, with any people, Sequoyah would have been considered a genius. He was an expert painter and silversmith. More important, he performed one of the most amazing feats in human history. Sequoyah knew that, thanks to their written language, whites could relay their words over a long distance. He became intrigued with letters and books, the white men's "talking leaves."[1]

According to one story, a nephew boasted to Sequoyah how smart he was, because he learned to read and write at a white man's school. Sequoyah, irritated by this braggart, said that Indians could read and write in their own language if they so chose. He then began a 12-year project, interrupted only by service in the Creek War—the creation of an alphabet of the Cherokee language.

Sequoyah started off with a major handicap. Since he neither read nor wrote English, he knew nothing of alphabets. At first he identified each Cherokee word by a pictoral symbol. That led to too many symbols. He decided, then, to sort out the words by sounds.

Like many geniuses, Sequoyah was not appreciated by everybody while completing his work. He ignored his farm to concentrate on the alphabet. Many thought him crazy or even touched by witchcraft. His wife badgered him so much that he moved to an isolated cabin. But even the change of workplace would not bring him peace; neighbors burned down his cabin.[2]

Sequoyah displays the alphabet he developed in order to write the Cherokee language.

In 1821, Sequoyah revealed his new alphabet. Some of the symbols he used were copied from an English spelling book. Some were Greek letters, and some were original symbols he invented. The English symbols, however, did not correspond to English letters. Sequoyah's alphabet used the *D* symbol, for instance, to represent the sound of the English letter *A*.

Sequoyah completed his task while visiting in Arkansas. The result proved wildly successful. Schoolchildren learned the new alphabet in only two days. Adults in the West could write letters to their families and friends in the East. Sequoyah carried some of those letters with him on his trip East. He planned to teach the alphabet to the Cherokee Nation.

He had to convince his eastern tribesmen of the invention's value. First he gathered some of the brightest youths and taught them the alphabet. Then he assembled them before the tribal leaders. Sequoyah dictated a message, and the youngsters copied exactly the same message.

The chiefs were convinced. Sequoyah, until recently considered an eccentric, was now a hero. No other person in the recorded history of the world had invented an alphabet by him- or herself. Sequoyah's alphabet brought a new sense of unity and pride to the Cherokees. Now they could communicate in their own language over hundreds of miles, on a level equal to or better than that of whites.

For many Cherokees, Sequoyah's alphabet was not their first experience with a written language. A religious group known as the Moravians had established a school for the Cherokees in 1801. The Cherokees had hesitated to welcome these missionaries, because they did not want to change their religion. But they were eager for book learning. They allowed the Moravians into the Nation—if the missionaries agreed to teach in the schools and refrain from preaching.

Gradually, the missionaries gained the Cherokees' trust. They even converted many Indians to Christianity. Much-respected Chief Charles Hicks was baptized in 1813. Others followed his example. In times to come, missionaries would bring more than religion and education to the Cherokees. They would become some of the Nation's staunchest allies in their conflict with the American government.

By 1826, there were 18 missions scattered throughout the Cherokee Nation teaching girls as well as boys. Moravian, Presbyterian, and Methodist churches footed part of the schools' bills. So did the federal government, because an educated Indian was less likely to be a warlike one. Several of the students continued their education beyond the elementary level. A mission-based school in Cornwall, Connecticut, taught students from around the world. Cherokees in the school gained a reputation for their academic ability.

One of those students was John Ridge, son of The Ridge. Another

A Moravian missionary addresses a group of Cherokees.

was his cousin, Elias Boudinot. In later years they would be controversial Cherokee leaders. In the 1820s, both were love-struck students, whose romances indirectly led to the downfall of their school.

John Ridge suffered a hip infection during his second year at the school. While recovering, he stayed at the home of school official John Northrup. He recovered from his injury. But the love bug bit, and he never recovered from that. He met, and fell in love with, Northrup's daughter Sara. Her parents tried to separate the young couple. They sent Sara to stay with her grandmother, and John Ridge went home to finish his recuperation.

John Ridge returned to New England in style. He and The Ridge rode into Cornwall in a splendid coach drawn by four white horses. The dignified Ridge showed the Northrups that their daughter was marrying into a wealthy family.

The parents approved the marriage of their daughter to a Cherokee, but some townspeople were enraged. The newspaper editor of a neighboring town wrote that "some [people of Cornwall] have said that the girl ought to be publicly whipped, the Indian hung, and the mother drowned."[3] Missionaries, the editor charged, were responsible for the scandal. Mission leaders made no attempt to refute such bigotry. Instead, noted clergyman Lyman Beecher issued a public statement deploring interracial marriage.[4]

Elias Boudinot and 19-year-old Harriet Gold suffered even more than John Ridge and Sara Northrup. Boudinot graduated from the mission school and attended college in Andover, Massachusetts. Harriet, the daughter of a prosperous farmer and merchant, told her parents that she wanted to become a missionary and marry Boudinot. The shocked parents adamantly opposed her wishes. Harriet became ill and grew worse every day. Her parents feared for her life. To give her an incentive to recover, they agreed to the marriage.

Townspeople went out of their way to make the young couple miserable. Girls in the church choir wore black armbands. Harriet received hate letters. The church bell rang in funereal tones. The night before the wedding, a mob burned Harriet Gold, her mother, and Boudinot in effigy. The mob included Harriet's brothers. No one came to her defense.[5]

Instead of marrying in the hostile church, Boudinot and Gold exchanged vows in her parents' home. Then they left Cornwall, never to return. Boudinot learned from this marriage that whites, even those who professed admiration for the Cherokees, would not accept them as equals.

The funeral bells at the church sounded the death of Cornwall's mission school. Racked by the "scandal" of the marriages, it closed in 1827.

Harriet Boudinot's future was much brighter than her wedding would indicate. The pleasant rolling hills of the Cherokee lands reminded her of New England. The house she and her wealthy husband shared was comfortable and well furnished. She enjoyed the intellectual company both of white missionaries and of Cherokees. Her parents came to visit. The home and people impressed them.

Elias Boudinot also led a fulfilling life. He would be one of the most influential Cherokees during the Nation's Golden Age.

Some people wondered why Sequoyah had bothered to create an alphabet. After all, the Cherokees could learn and use the English alphabet. But Sequoyah had felt that the Cherokees could never achieve true independence if they relied upon the communication system of another culture.

Boudinot was an excellent person to help spread that culture. The Cherokees, he believed, needed a newspaper. With the help of missionary Samuel Worcester, he created that paper.

The Cherokee Tribal Council issued Boudinot money for a printing press. He went North to secure more funds. Boudinot persuaded investors that the Cherokees were "industrious and intelligent people."[6] An 1825 census showed the prosperous tribe's change from warlike hunters to southern farmers. The Cherokees boasted 22,000 cattle, 7,600 horses, 46,000 swine, 2,500 sheep, 762 looms, 2,488 spinning wheels, 172 wagons, 2,943 plows, 10 sawmills, 331 grist-mills, 62 blacksmith shops, 8 cotton machines, 18 ferries, and 18 schools.

They were similar to white southerners in another way. At first, freed blacks and escaped slaves lived peaceably in the Cherokee Nation. But as the Cherokees adopted the southern style of farming, they also introduced the evil institution of slavery. The census showed 1,277 slaves among the 17,000 people living in the Cherokee Nation.

The Cherokees adopted American-style government as well as American agriculture. They had a two-house legislature. Executive power lay with a principal chief elected to a four-year term. They had a Supreme Court, circuit courts, and district courts. Even the preamble of their constitution was similar to that of the American document.

Other changes reflected American government of the times. Women lost their right to vote. Citizenship was limited to free Cherokee males over 25. Cherokees with any African-American blood were not allowed to vote.

There was one main difference between the two nations. While the

United States government declared no national religion, the Cherokees proclaimed themselves a "Christian nation."

The Council voted in 1825 to build a permanent capital, which they called New Echota, on land claimed by Georgia. Only Rev. Worcester, newspaper editor Boudinot, and the paper's printer had permanent homes there. But New Echota had the Council House, a Supreme Court building, a print shop, taverns, and stores for legislators and judges when the Council met. Cherokee leaders planned for New Echota to be the intellectual as well as political capital of the Cherokee Nation. The Council proposed a National Academy with classrooms, lecture halls, a library, reading rooms, natural history displays, historical exhibits, and a museum of arts and crafts.

In 1826, Boudinot raised enough money to order a printing press from a Boston company. When it arrived in New Echota, the newspaper readied for publication. It was called the *Cherokee Phoenix*; Worcester suggested the title. The phoenix was a mythical bird that rose from the ashes of its dying parent. Worcester compared the Cherokees' change in culture to a rebirth from the ashes of the past. The paper also had a title in the Cherokee language, with words that translated "I will arise."[7]

The first edition of the *Cherokee Phoenix* appeared on February 21, 1828. Boudinot's opening editorial called for peace between Cherokees and whites. He hoped for "that happy period…when the terms 'Indian depredations,' 'war whoop,' 'scalping knife,' and the like shall become obsolete and for ever be 'buried under deep ground.'"[8]

Boudinot's newspaper, printed in both Cherokee and English, contained their constitution, Cherokee laws, and even the Lord's Prayer. It also included articles about such topics as the benefits of laughter, excavations of the ancient Roman city of Pompeii, and the possible collision between earth and a comet.

Interest in the *Phoenix* spread far beyond the Nation's boundaries. Farmers in Tennessee read it. So did missionaries in New England, senators in Washington, D.C., and state officials in Georgia. The well-written Cherokee newspaper represented a proud and determined people—a people determined to remain in their ancestral home.

Chapter 5

"Never Again to Cede One More Foot of Our Land"

By 1820, Britain posed no danger to the United States. Napoleon was stopped, and France was a defeated nation. Spain still owned Florida, but that hold was weak. Americans had freed their soil from the threat of Europeans. Now they could concentrate on evicting Indians.

The United States had the power to oust Native Americans by force. The 1820 U.S. census showed 10 million Americans; Georgia alone had nearly 3 million. The entire Cherokee Nation had only about 15,000 people. More important, the U.S. Army had guns and ammunition. The Cherokees had spinning wheels and plows. Yet most Americans had little or no desire to fight the Indians.

Likewise, the Cherokees and other tribes wanted to avoid violence with Americans. Some Cherokees wanted statehood. Others would settle for being a district, much like the District of Columbia. Above all, they wanted freedom and sovereignty over their land. Many whites were not willing to honor this wish.

Of all the states, Georgia was the most bothered by the Cherokee presence. The Cherokee Nation also had lands in Tennessee, North Carolina, and Alabama, but two-thirds of the Nation lay within Georgia. Both the state and the Nation were claiming the same territory. Furthermore, Georgians remembered the 1802 agreement to remove Indians from the state's lands as soon as "peaceably" possible. Georgia was not alone. As new states entered the union, each wanted the right to oust its resident Indians.

Sequoyah could invent an alphabet. Boudinot could publish a high-quality newspaper. Other Cherokees could form a government based on the U.S. model. But to the southerners who coveted the land where Cherokees and other Native Americans resided, Indians would always be inferior and should be driven out. If anything, the Cherokees' adoption of the white man's ways only hastened the whites' desire to evict them. Racists could easily justify to themselves their opinion that Cherokees were uncivilized savages, when Indian culture (whatever its true nature) appeared different from white culture. But when Cherokee culture began more closely to resemble the European-American culture, racists felt threatened: Perhaps the Cherokees were superior to whites—all the more reason to get rid of them.

Whites could not evict the Cherokees by law. John Marshall, Chief Justice of the U.S. Supreme Court, often sided with the Indians. An 1821 decision from the Supreme Court ruled that they had a right to do with their land as they saw fit and that Congress could not steal it.

Secretary of War John C. Calhoun, to appease the Georgians, requested that a group of Cherokee leaders meet in Washington. The Cherokees said that if the U.S. government wanted to talk with them, they could meet at the tribe's annual Council meeting.

Hundreds of Cherokees gathered for the 1823 Council. It took 30 cooks to prepare the beef, venison, pork, fowl, and baked goods for the meetings. Commissioners urged the Cherokees to yield their eastern lands in exchange for new lands in the West. The Cherokees replied, "It is our fixed and unalterable determination of this Nation never again to cede one more foot of our land."[1]

William McIntosh, a chief of the now-friendly Creeks, was sent by the U.S. government to talk with Cherokee leaders after the meeting. They agreed to meet with him—as long as everything McIntosh said was put in writing.

McIntosh offered bribes—including $2,000 to John Ross—"as presents, $12,000 you can divide among your friends." Ross read the bribe offer to the full Council and commented, "Fortunately, the author has mistaken my character and my sense of honor."[2] The embarrassed American delegate left.

Two years later the Cherokees strengthened their intention to hold

Supreme Court Chief Justice John Marshall angered many people by siding with the Indians in matters regarding their rights.

their land. The tribe declared at the 1825 Council that all lands in the Nation were under control of the Nation. They added this rule to prevent corrupt chiefs from yielding to bribery.

Cherokee delegations eventually did go to Washington to present their case for keeping their land. Ross told President James Monroe, "The Cherokees are not foreigners, but the original inhabitants of America, and that they now stand on the soil of their own territory, and they cannot recognize the sovereignty of any state within the limits of their territory."[3]

William McIntosh, the chief of the Creeks who was sent by the U.S. government to bribe Cherokee leaders into surrendering their tribal lands

President Monroe's successor, John Quincy Adams, proclaimed a "higher obligation" to respect the Indians' rights. When Ross, The Ridge, Chief George Lowrey, and Elijah Hicks, son of former chief Charles Hicks, met him, he remarked that their manners were those of "well-bred gentlemen."[4] Yet President Adams on other occasions commented that the Indians were savages and Marshall was a fool.[5] Early in his term, Adams signed treaties with several other tribes for their emigration. He had no objection to persuading Cherokees to leave their lands.

President John Quincy Adams, while stating that he respected the rights of American Indians, also actively encouraged their removal.

Georgia congressmen scowled at the kind treatment the Cherokees received in the capital. One called them "savages subsisting upon wild herbs and disgusting reptiles." The Cherokees heard this insult. During a state dinner, Lowrey saw a waiter with a dish of sweet potatoes. Lowrey shouted for the waiter to bring him the food, then thanked him for "these roots. We Indians are very fond of roots," Lowrey proclaimed, as other guests laughed at the Georgians.[6]

When the Cherokees adopted their constitution in 1827, Georgia saw a threat to its power. The Cherokee document was a violation of Article IV of the U.S. Constitution, state leaders claimed. That article read, "No new state will be formed or erected within the jurisdiction of any other state...without the consent of the legislature of the states concerned as well as that of Congress." When Georgia governor John Forsythe read the Cherokee constitution in the *Cherokee Phoenix,* he sent a copy of the newspaper to President Adams and demanded his support.

Georgians initiated their own campaign to force the Cherokees from their lands. The legislature resolved in late 1827:

> [T]hat all the lands, appropriated and unappropriated, which lie within the conventional limits of Georgia belong to her absolutely...that the Indians are tenants at her will...and that Georgia has the right to extend her authority and her laws over the whole territory and to coerce obedience to them from all descriptions of people...who may reside within her limits.[7]

Wilson Lumpkin, a Georgia congressman, brought the matter to Congress. His December 1827 resolution read: "Resolved, that the Committee on Indian Affairs be instructed to inquire into the expediency of providing, by law, for the removal of the various tribes of Indians who have located within the States and Territories of the United States to some eligible solution, west of the Mississippi River."[8]

President Adams sent a representative to talk with the Cherokees but took no further action. Indian removal was not his primary concern. He faced a tough reelection challenge in 1828 from his 1824 foe, Andrew Jackson. Cherokees may have been critical of Adams's indecisiveness, but Jackson as president could only be worse. The former Indian fighter made removal of Indians from eastern lands a campaign promise.

Few doubted the outcome of the election. Massachusetts native Adams carried the northeastern states, but "Old Hickory"—a nickname given Jackson because of his hardness—won by a landslide elsewhere.

Although several Indian delegations from various tribes went to Washington over the years to meet with government leaders, few succeeded in negotiating the right to keep their tribal lands.

During his term in office, the Cherokee issue would have an impact on the entire government: the duties of the president, the powers of the Supreme Court, the responsibilities of Congress, and the balance of powers between the federal and state governments.

There was another important election in 1828. John Ross became chief of the Cherokee Nation in October. He and Jackson would be less-than-friendly adversaries for the next ten years. The men provided a startling contrast. Ross, only 38 years old, was 15 years younger than his American counterpart. Short, stocky Ross kept his temper as often as long, lean Jackson lost his. They shared one characteristic: the love and admiration of the common people they led.

Immediately, Jackson fulfilled the Cherokees' worst nightmares. Not only did he encourage Georgia's expulsion efforts, but he also urged Alabama to do the same. His first major legislative proposal called for Indian removal. The Removal Bill, as it was called, demanded "that it shall and may be lawful for the United States...to cause so much of any territory...west of the Mississippi for the reception of such tribes or nations of Indians as may choose to exchange lands where they now reside."[9] The bill also gave the president the power to aid the Native Americans in their move and allowed $500,000 to pay for such a move.

The only other issue that would split the nation like the proposed ouster of Indians from eastern lands would be slavery. Friends and neighbors argued with a passion. The Cherokees and other tribes found allies throughout the United States, particularly among white missionaries in the North. One of them, Jeremiah Evarts, led the opposition to the Removal Bill. Evarts had studied and knew Indian history thoroughly and became an expert in the legal rights of the Cherokees.

Evarts crusaded for the Cherokees in essays written under the name William Penn. One essay commented:

> If the Cherokee should make war upon the United States, they might then, by the laws of nations, be treated as a conquered people....But so long as the Cherokees act in a peaceful manner, it would be barbarous in the extreme to treat them as a conquered people. I speak without any reference to treaties, and on the supposition that we were bound only by the common obligations of justice and humanity.[10]

The "William Penn" essays had two main themes: first, that the Cherokees had an indisputable right to the land; and second, that mass removal to the West could only hurt the tribe. Either they would be sent to worthless lands and perish, or they would be moved to desirable lands that Americans sooner or later would claim.

The Cherokees had adopted white men's ways. They showed remarkable ability to learn the white man's culture, religion, and agriculture. Along with the Creeks, Choctaws, Chickasaws, and Seminoles, they were known to both white Americans and Native Americans as the "Five Civilized Tribes." In reality, of course, the Indians had long been "civilized" people.

Now Cherokees and their white allies both asked why the government was pressuring Cherokees to abandon their lands. They had assumed that if Cherokees acted like whites, then whites would treat them with respect and accept them as equals, worthy of having their own nation and being neighbors. One Cherokee declared:

> The Indians say they don't know how to understand their Father the President. A few years ago he sent them a plough and a hoe—said it was not good for his red children to hunt—they must cultivate the earth. Now he tells them there is good hunting at the Arkansas; if they go there he will give them rifles.[11]

Even former frontiersmen spoke out in favor of the Indians. Sam Houston, who had lived among the Cherokees, said of them, "These Indians are not inferior to white men. John Ridge is not inferior in point of genius to John Randolph," a noted Virginia senator.[12]

Andrew Jackson did not share Houston's opinion of the Cherokees. Jackson argued that they "have neither the intelligence, the industry, the moral habits, nor the desire for improvement. Established in the midst of another and superior race...they must necessarily yield...and ere long disappear." He advised the Georgia legislature, "Build a fire under them. When it gets hot enough, they'll move."[13]

The legislature took Jackson's hint. Late in 1829, the state passed a series of laws that took away many of the Cherokees' rights and freedoms. Georgia confiscated all Cherokee lands and nullified all Cherokee laws in those lands. The state prohibited further meetings of the Cherokee Legislative Council. It called for arrest and imprisonment of any Cherokee who influenced tribesmen to resist emigration. Contracts between Cherokees and whites were illegal unless witnessed by two whites. Cherokees could no longer testify against Americans in Georgia courts.

The Georgia laws added to a storm of controversy about Cherokee rights that was already sweeping across the nation. Cherokees regularly sent messages known as memorials to influence congressional action. Some congressmen listened.

Senators and congressmen exchanged fiery oratory on both sides of the Removal Bill. In opposition to the bill, Senator Theodore Frelinghuysen of New Jersey declared:

> God in his providence planted these tribes on this western continent, so far as we know, before Great Britain herself had a political existence….The Indians are justly entitled to a share in the common bounties of a benignant Providence. And with this conceded, I ask in what code of the law of nations, or by what process of abstract deduction, their rights have been extinguished….Do the obligations of justice change with the color of the skin?…Our fathers…successfully and triumphantly contended for the very rights and privileges that our Indian neighbors now implore us to protect and preserve in them.[14]

He proposed an amendment designed to protect the Indians:

> Until…said tribes or nations shall choose to remove, as by this act is contemplated, they shall be protected, in their present possessions, and in the enjoyment of all their rights of territory, and government, as heretofore exercised and enjoyed, from all interruptions and encroachments.[15]

The Senate rejected Frelinghuysen's amendment, 27–20. The vote went along sectional lines. New England's senators favored it 11–1, but all 18 southern senators opposed it. The final vote on the bill was similar to the vote on the amendment.

The Senate added a phrase meant to soothe some opponents. It read, "Nothing in this act shall be considered as authorizing the violation of any existing treaty between the United States and the various Indian tribes." Despite these soothing words, however, the law was clearly a violation of existing treaties, which granted the land to the Cherokees forever.[16]

The vote was closer in the House of Representatives. The bill passed, 102–97. President Jackson, who had spent 17 years trying to expel Indians from eastern lands, signed it immediately.

Even after this defeat, the Cherokees continued their appeals to the nation's conscience. Articles in the *Phoenix* appeared throughout America and Europe. Their memorials were ignored by the Jackson administration, but not by Jackson's foes.

The plea was fervent, but the tone was doubtful. On July 17, 1830, the Cherokees appealed:

> We wish to remain on the land of our fathers. We have a perfect and original right to remain without interruption or molestation. The treaties with us, and laws of the United States made in pursuance of treaties, guarantee our residence and our privileges. Our only request is that these treaties be fulfilled, and these laws executed....We make this, perhaps our last appeal, to the good people of the United States.[17]

Chapter 6

"A Permanent Home...
Theirs Forever"

Cherokee legend described the West as a place ruled by evil, so treacherous that even the sun died. According to a tribal story, a party of Cherokee warriors and their families went West, never to return, doomed to wander endlessly and hopelessly in the darkness.[1]

Despite these reported perils of the West, some Cherokees willingly made the trip. Often they found hardships similar to the ones their brothers and sisters faced in the East.

The first recorded westward migration took place in 1794, the year before the Treaty of Holston. A Cherokee named Boul, during a guerrilla scuffle with whites, met a party of 6 white men, 3 white women, 4 white children, and 21 black slaves. He killed the white men and captured the others.

Boul feared his fellow Cherokees would turn him over to the whites. He, his followers, and the captives migrated to Texas and started a colony there. The Cherokees found a land similar to that which their ancestors knew. In the East, even in 1794, increasing numbers of whites and their gradual destruction of the forest were making game scarce. West of the Mississippi River, Boul saw buffalo herds that no longer existed in the East. Elk, deer, jackrabbits, prairie dogs, squirrels, and rabbits would provide plentiful food. The high grasses teemed with turkeys and prairie chickens. Golden eagles soared in the skies. Whippoorwills sang in the twilight. Migrating geese paraded through the air twice a year. Catfish abounded in streams and lakes, inviting people to catch and eat them. The rolling Ozark Mountains reminded the Cherokees of their hilly land back home.

For the Cherokees, leaving their homelands to begin new lives in the West was a painful experience.

The large herds of buffalo roaming western lands provided transplanted Cherokees with various necessities, including food and clothing.

Another group of renegades headed West in 1808. Chickamaugans, descendants of the followers of the unsuccessful Dragging Canoe, failed to make peace with their tribesmen. President Thomas Jefferson suggested to them that if they could not get along with their fellow Cherokees, they should leave the Nation. He even offered them land in the West. More than 1,100 Cherokees accepted the offer. They would be known as the Old Settlers by the generations who followed them.

Two years later, a Cherokee named Duwali led 75 men from their village to the West. In later years, he would become the most important of the western chiefs. But now he was considered a traitor. The Cherokee National Council had denounced him for accepting a land offer by the U.S. government and moving without the Cherokee government's permission. He and his villagers hunted, traded, and raided in present-day Arkansas, Louisiana, and Texas.

The eastern Cherokee Nation had reason to worry about westward migration. Fewer tribe members meant less power and influence for the Cherokee Nation in its negotiations with the United States.

A painting by American artist Winslow Homer depicts Indians making a canoe.

Western Cherokees gave their eastern kin cause to worry. In exchange for a permanent reserve in the northern Arkansas territory, the westerners gave up claims to land rights in the East. At this time, in 1817, Western Cherokees numbered about 3,000.

The long-deceased Attakullakulla would have more easily recognized the transplanted western Cherokees than those who remained in the eastern Nation. Unlike the eastern Cherokees with their Council and constitution, the western settlers kept a more decentralized government. Each village was a separate political entity that sent one or more representatives to intervillage community councils. Within each village were a "white" (peacetime) chief and a "red" (wartime) one. The red organization also went on diplomatic missions headed by warriors.

The western Cherokees lived in rectangular houses, usually made of logs, about 16 feet (5 meters) wide and 60 feet (18 meters) long. A village consisted of 30 to 80 houses, built near cultivated fields. Councils met in a central town house.

Ceremonies remained important to the western Cherokees, more

so than to the easterners. Nature and the heavens had to be kept in har-
mony in this still-unfamiliar land. The cold months, October through April,
were the times for major ceremonies. Cherokees celebrated the creation of
the world with ritual bathing, hunting, and fasting, followed by a huge
feast. The warm season, May through September, was the time for war and
farming. Women tended fields and wove cloth. They, along with children
and the elderly, gathered fruits, nuts, and berries. Men took part in raid-
ing their enemies. In their free time, men competed in ball games.

The U.S. government promised that the Cherokees could live in the
western lands. The Osage, who already lived there, had different ideas.
Cherokees pushed into the lands of the Osage, and the Osage retaliated.
Blood flowed on both sides. Eastern tribe members had abolished the old
law of vengeance that required a Cherokee to avenge a kinsman's death
by members of another tribe, but western Cherokees continued the violent
custom against the Osage and other tribes as well.

The U.S. government ultimately settled the Cherokee–Osage fight.
The Osage were offered reparations if they would give up claims to Cherokee land. This peacemaking came with a price. The government said it
could not protect the western Cherokees unless easterners were willing to
yield a corresponding amount of land. The irate eastern Cherokee chiefs
refused the deal, but the government found corrupt Cherokees willing to
sign the necessary papers in exchange for a bribe.

With the Osage gone, the western Cherokees could settle down.
Like their eastern brothers and sisters, they prospered. By 1819, about 6,000
Cherokees lived in the Arkansas territory.[2]

Whites as well as Indians decided to take their chances with the
still-unknown land. Their government would not or could not stop them.
These new settlers cleared the land, causing game to disappear once more.
Once again, immigrating whites felt there was not enough room in the
same territory for them and the Cherokees. In 1828, whites prevailed. The
federal government arranged a treaty with the Cherokees. The western
Cherokees would give up their claims to Arkansas lands for lands farther
west in Oklahoma, which would be "a permanent home...which shall,
under the most solemn guarantee of the United States, be and remain theirs
forever."[3]

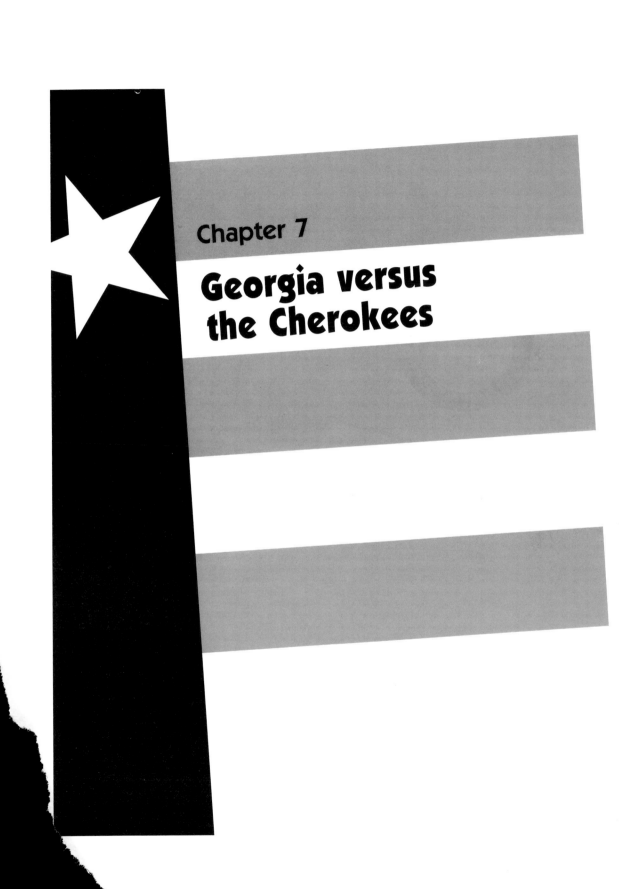

Chapter 7

Georgia versus the Cherokees

O n June 30, 1830, gold was discovered in the Georgia Cherokee hills. More than 10,000 gold seekers poured into the Cherokee Nation. They would find $16.5 million in gold, the second-richest deposit in North America at the time.

The gold seekers brought terror with them. Those who did not find gold began stealing Cherokee land, seizing livestock, ousting Cherokees from their homes, and assaulting owners who resisted. The Georgia government offered no support to the Cherokees. In fact, soldiers ordered them from the gold fields. Jackson sent federal troops to stop the property seizures and assaults, but withdrew them at the request of the Georgia governor. Instead the Georgia guard was brought in, a group who sometimes behaved little better than thieves, yet enjoyed legal authority.

Eastern Cherokees were determined to hold their ground. They saw the 1828 treaty between their western brethren and the U.S. government and realized that no land promised by the American government would be "permanent." John Ross and other leaders knew that only by remaining a unified, disciplined nation with nonviolent resistance would they have any chance to remain in their home. The tribe, despite many humiliations and bribes from whites, remained firm in its devotion to Ross.

The federal government made moves intended to cripple the Cherokees. Annuities of $6,000 paid to the tribe for previous land cessions were halted. Rules outlawing the sale of liquor to the Cherokees were revoked, encouraging addiction to alcohol. Spies were enlisted to spread rumors in Cherokee councils.

Georgia passed a law declaring it illegal to prevent or deter any Indian from selling or ceding any property to the United States for the use of Georgia. Another law prevented Indians from giving up property anywhere except to the state of Georgia. This kept them from selling to sympathetic whites who would let them stay on the land.

The state also banned Indian political gatherings except for the purpose of land cessions. Since the Cherokee capital of New Echota was located in northern Georgia, the tribe was forced to hold its meetings elsewhere.

Jeremiah Evarts, in one of his "William Penn" essays, suggested that "the Cherokees had better stand up to their arms" or "be trampled as the serfs of Georgia."[1] The tribe listened. They strengthened the powers of their chiefs to deal on the renewal issue and to pay any necessary legal fees.

Evarts advised John Ross to tell President Jackson that the United States was bound to protect Cherokee rights against Georgia. The Cherokees should not think of a treaty until they got assurance of their rights. Any treaty must be made by the Cherokees *as a Nation* with the approval of the majority of the Nation. Intruders should be kept off Cherokee lands.[2]

Now Ross had to decide his course of action. It appeared obvious that two of the three branches of American government were against him. The executive branch, in the person of President Andrew Jackson, made no secret of its desire for Indian removal. Jackson's cabinet officers refused to meet with the Cherokees for any reason other than to discuss a move west. The legislative branch, Congress, had already passed the Removal Bill. That meant the Cherokees' only hope lay with the judicial branch, the court system.

The Cherokees hired one of the nation's best lawyers, William Wirt of Baltimore. Wirt suggested that the tribe find a test case and take it to the Supreme Court. One such case soon appeared. A Cherokee named Corn Tassel was accused of murdering another Cherokee on Nation land claimed by Georgia. Corn Tassel was condemned to death by a Georgia court.

Cherokee leaders argued that Corn Tassel's fate was the Cherokee

Lawyer William Wirt unsuccessfully represented the Cherokees before the Supreme Court.

Nation's business, not Georgia's. The U.S. Supreme Court agreed, but Georgia ignored a Supreme Court order and hanged the hapless man.

Georgia Governor Wilson Lumpkin then wrote to President Jackson, "It appears to me that the rulers of the Cherokees have sufficient intelligence to see the utter imbecility of placing any further reliance upon the Supreme Court to sustain their pretensions....Georgia is not account-able to the Supreme Court or any other tribunal on earth."[3]

Wirt, however, was only beginning his fight. He brought up another case against the state of Georgia. The Cherokees were an inde-pendent nation and not subject to Georgia laws, he argued. Thus the Supreme Court was correct in its order to the state not to execute Corn Tassel.

Justice John Smith Thompson noted that treaties were signed with the Cherokees, just as they were with any other foreign nation. By these treaties, the Cherokees had the right to occupy and rule their lands.

Justice Thompson was overruled. Even Chief Justice John Marshall, usually a friend of the Cherokees, went against the tribe. Marshall stated, "An Indian tribe or nation within the United States is not a foreign state in the sense of the Constitution, and cannot maintain an action in the courts of the United States."[4]

Encouraged by their Supreme Court victory, Georgia politicians enacted even more outrageous laws. The legislature passed a bill ordering Cherokee land divided into 160-acre lots. The state held a lottery and distributed the land to white Georgians.

Cherokees were not the only victims of Georgia laws. Non-Cherokees who supported them also faced the wrath of Georgia authori-ties. Missionaries who urged opposition were some of the major obstacles to relocation. Many Georgians saw the missionaries as irritating intruders who meddled in problems of no concern to them. Georgia passed a law on December 22, 1830, providing that no white person could reside in Chero-kee country located in Georgia without a license from the governor. That license would be given only if the person was willing to swear an oath of loyalty to the state of Georgia. A party led by The Ridge went to Wash-ington to seek repeal of the Georgia law. Secretary of War John Henry Eaton told them the only delegation of Cherokees he would see was one that had "written authority to discuss a removal treaty."[5]

The Georgia law took effect March 1, 1831. Eleven days later, mis-sionaries Samuel Worcester, Isaac Proctor, and Jack Thompson were arrested. All were released on a technicality. Since all three were postmas-ters paid by federal funds, they were federal employees and not subject to the Georgia law. Secretary of War Eaton raged when he heard of the dismissal, because he wanted Cherokee allies out of the Cherokee lands. He saw to it that all three were fired from their postmaster jobs.

The Georgia militia returned that July and arrested ten missionaries plus the printer of the *Cherokee Phoenix,* a white man. These prisoners were treated with deliberate brutality, and the ministers were even forbidden to hold services while in jail.

All 11 defendants were tried on September 15, 1831. Nine of them, believing they would not receive a fair trial, gave up and signed the loyalty oath. Only missionaries Samuel Worcester and Elizur Butler continued to defy the Georgia government. Both were found guilty and sentenced to four years of hard labor.

The convictions aroused heated protests throughout the country. This was not merely a question of Cherokee rights. The missionaries were American citizens, who supposedly could live where they pleased without swearing oaths to governments. Clergymen, writers, and politicians, particularly in the North, denounced the Georgians. The American Board of Commissioners for Foreign Missions made a formal protest to President Jackson. The president used the excuse that he had no right to interfere in a state's government.

Wirt and the Cherokees, meanwhile, started their own defense of the missionaries. They filed a lawsuit, *Worcester v. Georgia,* which charged that Worcester was a guest of the Cherokees and Georgia had no right to arrest him. On March 3, 1832, the Supreme Court made its decision. Chief Justice Marshall himself wrote the opinion: "The acts of Georgia are repugnant to the Constitution, laws and treaties of the United States....The forcible seizure and abduction of the plaintiff in error...is...a violation."[6]

An elated Elias Boudinot wrote to his cousin, Stand Watie, "It is glorious news...a great triumph on the part of the Cherokees....The question is forever settled who is right and who is wrong."[7]

Any Cherokee victory celebration was short-lived. Jackson immediately gave notice that he would not follow the court's order. "John Marshall has made his decision," Jackson declared. "Now let him enforce it."[8]

Chapter 8

"Get the Indians Out of Georgia, Sir!"

The Supreme Court victory for the two missionaries, Worcester and Butler, meant nothing. Both remained in a Georgia jail cell. Butler worked as a cobbler and Worcester as a carpenter. If anything, the Supreme Court decision strengthened Georgia Governor Lumpkin's resolve. He declared, "Any attempt to influence the evident right of a state to govern the entire population within its territorial limits and to punish all offenses committed against its laws . . . would be usurpation of a power never granted by the states."[1]

Worcester and Butler remained in jail for nearly a year. The Mission Board finally told Worcester to give up his lawsuit, which he did, and both were freed. The missionaries could claim a moral victory, because they had won their Supreme Court case. The Cherokees were happy to see them. But Georgia won the real victory: No power, not even the federal government, could prevent the state from ousting Native Americans.

John Ridge spent the spring of 1832 touring the North. He hoped his speeches and lectures would bring public support and funds to his people. On the way home, he stopped in Washington and met with President Jackson. Ridge asked Jackson if he would support federal action against Georgia's attempts at Indian removal. Jackson said he would not.

The meeting affected Ridge. Jackson adviser Amos Kendall noted, "From that moment he was convinced that the only alternative to save his people from moral and physical death was to make the best terms they could with the government, and remove out of the limits of the states."[2]

Ridge returned home and discussed the matter with his father. The

Ridge, who had once killed a tribesman who attempted to sell Cherokee land, was convinced by his son's argument to support negotiations for removal. John Ridge also convinced his influential cousins, Elias Boudinot and Stand Watie.

Flaring tempers made the 1832 Council meeting at Red Clay, Tennessee, hotter than the July 23 temperature. John Ross's opening address served as a warning to those who would give up Cherokee lands. He declared, "A man who will forsake his country in time of adversity and will co-operate with those who oppress his own kindred is no more than a traitor and should be viewed and shunned as such."[3]

Ross's speech failed to convince the Ridges, Boudinot, and Stand Watie. The Council accomplished nothing. The Cherokees decided not to hold their scheduled elections, because they feared reprisals from the Georgia government.

The antitreaty faction, led by Ross, still formed a huge majority of the Cherokees. This split led Boudinot to resign as editor of the *Phoenix*. Ross wanted the *Phoenix* to be a show of the Nation's unity. He would not permit Boudinot's pro-treaty views in the paper. Boudinot himself, in the first issue of the *Phoenix*, had declared: "We will invariably state the will of the majority of our people on the subject of the present controversy with Georgia, and the present removal policy of the United States government."[4] Now he no longer represented that majority.

Boudinot considered himself a realist, not a traitor. He felt the odds against his people were hopeless. "I have done what I could. I have served my country, I hope with fidelity," he told Ross.[5]

Elijah Hicks took over as the *Phoenix* editor. He was enthusiastic, but he lacked Boudinot's journalistic ability. The newspaper became little more than a home for antitreaty propaganda and soon suspended publication.

Ross and the antitreaty Cherokees held a keen interest in the 1832 American presidential election. Henry Clay, one of the Cherokees' strongest defenders in Congress, was the presidential nominee of the Whig party. Senators Daniel Webster and Theodore Frelinghuysen supported Clay. So did noted orator Edward Everett. So did former Indian fighters Sam Houston and Davy Crockett.

Most voters, however, stuck with Andrew Jackson, who was running for reelection. He received 707,000 votes, more than twice as many as his Whig opponent.

While the candidates were campaigning, lottery wheels were spinning in Georgia. The white Georgians who won this lucky sweepstakes would get Cherokee land, free. Jackson made no attempt to stop the giveaway. Shortly after Christmas, a stranger knocked on the door at the Cherokee Nation's Moravian mission. The caller announced he was the new owner of the property and demanded rent. The missionary slammed the door in his face, but the stranger soon came back with 18 of his friends and evicted the missionary.[6]

Similar scenes occurred throughout Cherokee Nation lands located within Georgia. Lottery winners and scoundrels took over farms, burned houses, attacked women, and even sold liquor in Cherokee churches.

If any event could have led to violence, it was this legalized robbery of Cherokee lands. Elijah Hicks in the *Phoenix* called it "one of the most shameless moral crimes that has ever been consummated in Christendom."[7] Yet the Cherokees responded peacefully to the atrocities heaped upon them.

Ross went to Washington again in early 1833. This time Jackson offered him $2.5 million plus replacement land in the West for the eastern Cherokee lands. When Ross made no reply, Jackson upped the price to $3 million. The gold fields alone are worth more than that, Ross answered. Besides, Ross said, "If you cannot protect us in the East, how can we believe that you will protect us in the West?"[8]

Later, Secretary of War Lewis Cass sent Ross a letter summarizing the government's offer. It offered the tribe western lands which would be theirs "forever." The letter concluded:

> I cannot but hope that you will see . . . the difficulties of your present situation....It is impossible you can remain where you are now and prosper. And if you persist in the effort, the time of regret will come, I am afraid, after the most injury to yourselves.[9]

John Ross, the Cherokee leader who fought for American Indian rights.

The Cherokees held a special Council meeting that April. Ross admitted no success in negotiating with Jackson but said that Jackson had ordered federal troops to keep peace on Cherokee lands. John Ridge spoke. The government was sending troops, he said. But those troops were going to Tennessee and North Carolina—not to violent Georgia. How did Ridge know this? Governor Lumpkin of Georgia told him.

Why was John Ridge talking with the man most detested by the Cherokees? Ridge's comment led to arguments between the Cherokee factions. Both sides soon realized that nothing further would be accomplished. They adjourned the Council and decided to return in October.

At the October meeting, John Ridge suggested sending a group to Washington to negotiate a removal treaty. The Council refused his motion. Instead, they sent a delegation led by Ross that would have no power to negotiate treaties. Ross, meanwhile, met with Secretary of War Cass and tried to reach a compromise. The Cherokees would give up some Georgia land if they could apply for U.S. citizenship. Cass responded that nothing short of complete removal was acceptable.

A large meteor shower passed through southern skies in November 1833. Many Cherokees interpreted the event as an omen of doom. Things looked bad for the Cherokees. They would only get worse.

Ross made another trip to Washington in early 1834. When he returned home, he found dozens of strangers on his property. They were the Georgians who had won his land in the lottery. His wife, Quatie, and their two children, while not evicted, were being held prisoner on the first floor of their home.

He and his family had no choice. They could not appeal in a Georgia court. They left their comfortable Georgia home with its barns, fields, and livestock and moved into a cabin in Tennessee. He found he was not alone. Every Council member loyal to him had been dispossessed.

Lands belonging to pro-treaty Cherokees remained untouched. In fact, they had received money from the government to rouse dissent. "Letters of protection" had saved the treaty advocates' property.

Some Cherokees gave up the fight. About 700 of them agreed to leave in 1834. Rev. Samuel Worcester, the missionary who was imprisoned for refusing to sign a loyalty oath, joined them. A peaceful and uneventful trip west might have encouraged other Cherokees to join them, but this party met a multitude of problems. Close confinement, liquor, and strange foods led to measles and other diseases. One boat sank beneath the Tennessee River. A woman preparing dinner fell overboard into the Mississippi. Rough waters on the Arkansas River forced the crew to throw valuable supplies overboard. Altogether, 81 persons died before reaching their destination. More than half those who perished were children.

When they got to Arkansas, a cholera epidemic killed 51 of the Cherokees. A doctor summoned from Little Rock, Arkansas, became exhausted from overwork. He, too, died of cholera. Half those who survived the journey were dead within a year.

Ross called another Council meeting for August. John Ridge once more pleaded his case. "We have no government. It is entirely suppressed," he said.[10]

Some Council members called for Ridge's impeachment. Ross stopped the motion but could not change the anger of treaty foes. A Ridge ally named James Walker was murdered on his way home. Jackson wrote Ross that from now on the Council would be held responsible if a Treaty supporter was killed.

Both parties returned for the October Council. Talk of impeachment stopped, but the Ridges demanded trials to clear their names. The Council majority refused. Both Ridges and Boudinot walked out of the Council and returned home. Now the Cherokees could not even pretend to be one Nation.

Although the majority of the Cherokee Nation still sided with Ross, Ridge predicted that he could produce a treaty in "one season" if he got "a hearty support from the states and the General Government."[11]

Treaty backers held a secret meeting November 13 at John Ridge's house. Two weeks later they formally organized the Treaty Party. The United States and Georgia governments immediately recognized the Party as the official representation of the Cherokee Nation.

Ridge went to Washington and presented his party's platform to Edward Everett. The influential senator was once a Ross ally, but Ridge's argument converted him. Everett commented that for a Cherokee, the choice was between moving West with his tribesmen and "sinking into a condition but little, if at all, better than slavery."[12]

President Jackson greeted the Treaty Party warmly but ignored Ross's faction. Ross, who also was in the capital, remained unconcerned, claiming the Senate would not ratify any treaty not approved by a majority of the Cherokees. He knew that most Cherokees stood behind him.

A huge, gruff commissioner named John Schermerhorn met with Ross. He repeated Jackson's offer—$3.5 million and western lands if the tribe moved. Ross countered with an offer he knew was ridiculous—$20 million. Schermerhorn suggested $4.5 million and additional western land. They parted without an agreement.

John Ridge gloated in a letter to his father:

> Ross has failed before the Senate, before the Secretary of War, and before the President. He tried hard to cheat you and his people, but he has been prevented....The United States will have nothing more to do with John Ross.[13]

Ridge and Schermerhorn signed a treaty in March 1835, although Ridge lacked the Cherokee authority to negotiate such a document. Ridge brought it back to the Cherokee Nation for approval. It offered money beyond the dreams of most of the tribe, yet Ridge was treated as an outcast. Ross, who came back with nothing, was called a hero for standing up to Jackson.

The Council met in May and refused even to consider the Ridge–Schermerhorn treaty. They cited numerous complaints from Cherokees who had moved to the Arkansas or Oklahoma territories. Even so, the U.S. government ordered census takers to count Cherokee property. Ross urged the Cherokees not to comply with these officials.

President Jackson told Schermerhorn to produce a treaty before the 1836 election. The wily commissioner came up with a loophole. Cherokee Council members had not been legally elected since 1828, and the Council was not legal. Therefore Ridge could form a Council of his own.

Ridge called a Council meeting in July. Ross urged his followers to attend it. Thousands of Cherokees, almost all of them removal opponents, showed up. They heard Schermerhorn, a man so hated he was nicknamed Skaynooyayanah ("Devil's horn"), attack Ross. Schermerhorn's rude behavior ruined any chance Ridge had to win the trust of his people.

A visitor came to see John Ross in the summer of 1835: John Henry Payne, a noted English author and playwright, who also had composed the song "Home, Sweet Home." Payne visited Ross to learn about his tribe's history. He first had visited John Ridge and Boudinot. Ridge called Ross "selfish, sordid, and violent." Payne, however, found Ross to be "mild, intelligent, and unaffected."[14] Ross invited him to stay and attend the October Council.

The writer was awed by the parade of Cherokees that passed by Ross's house. Groups of 30 to 50 men wore turbans and tunics with sashes. Some wore long robes. "They had the oriental air of the old scripture pictures of patriarchal processions," Payne wrote.[15]

He was equally impressed with Ross's calm leadership. The chief shook each member's hand and addressed him by name. When he spoke, all listened attentively. Payne realized the importance of the upcoming Council. He wrote: "All seem to contemplate the approaching meeting as one of vital impact. I myself, though a stranger, partake of the general excitement."[16]

At the October Council meeting, Superintendent of Indian Removal Benjamin Currey (a noted Indian foe), Colonel William Bishop of the Georgia Guard (a group Payne described as "more banditti than soldiers"[17]), and Schermerhorn represented the American government. They offered $3.25 million, plus $150,000 to settle back debts, plus 13 million acres of western land, plus an additional 800,000 acres, also in the West.

The Cherokees unanimously rejected the offer. Schermerhorn immediately raised the bid to $5 million. Again the Cherokees refused. Even the Ridges and Boudinot, perhaps fearing for their lives in this unfriendly gathering, voted against it.

Privately, they had different ideas. John Ridge wrote Georgia Governor Lumpkin, "The plan is in for a treaty in December." He closed the letter by adding: "My name must be reserved from the public eye."[18]

A few weeks after the October Council, two dozen Georgia guardsmen crossed the Tennessee state line. Without warning, they arrested Ross and Payne. When Payne asked what the charges were, one officer slapped him and told him, "You'll know soon enough."[19]

The two prisoners were thrown into a cabin that served as a jail. They had one disturbing "roommate." Hanging over them was the rotting corpse of a Cherokee who had been executed several weeks earlier.

President Martin Van Buren delivered the order that finally removed the Cherokees from their homelands.

Both were released within two weeks. Neither was charged with any crime. Instead of apologizing for the illegal arrest, Colonel Bishop of the Georgia Guard told Payne, "Now, sir! Cut out of Georgia. If you ever dare show your face in these territories, I'll make you curse the day you were born!"[20]

Schermerhorn still needed at least the pretense of a treaty. He called for a December Council meeting at the old capital of New Echota. Ross, now in Washington, advised his followers to boycott this meeting. Fewer than 500 Cherokees showed up for it.

Treaty opponents outnumbered advocates despite the boycott. The Treaty Party had a plan. A committee of 20 would negotiate a treaty. This took place at Boudinot's house, away from public scrutiny.

The treaty they signed was virtually the same one the Cherokees had refused in October. The Cherokees would get $5 million plus lands in the West, and the government would pay the removal expenses.

Only about 100 Cherokees signed the treaty. The Ridge was the last to put his name on the paper. He looked at it sadly and said, "I have signed my death warrant."[21]

The treaty enraged removal opponents throughout the United States. Former U.S. President John Quincy Adams called it "infamous. . . . It brings eternal disgrace upon the country."[22] William M. Davis, appointed by Secretary of War Cass to oversee the removal, said, "That paper . . . called a treaty, is no treaty at all, because it is not sanctioned by the great body of the Cherokees."[23]

Congressional leaders assured Ross that the treaty faced certain defeat in the Senate. Powerful congressional leaders such as Henry Clay, Daniel Webster, and John C. Calhoun told him not to worry. So did Senator Hugh Lawson White of Tennessee, chairman of the Committee on Indian Affairs.

The treaty passed by one vote—White's. The Tennessee senator never gave a reason for his change of mind.

Events beyond Ross's control hurt the Cherokees' cause. The Choctaws, Chickasaws, and Creeks had left their lands peacefully. But the Seminoles had hidden in Florida swamps and raided white settlements. Their aggressiveness had turned some whites against all Indians.

Northern senators helped pass the treaty for political reasons. New Yorker Martin Van Buren, running for president in place of the retiring Jackson, was not popular in the South. Northerners did not want to risk alienating southern voters by opposing the removal.[24]

Many Georgians acted as though the treaty gave them free rein in Cherokee lands. They ravaged properties of both removal advocates and opponents. Even treaty leader Boudinot complained that his estate was being invaded. John Ridge, the other treaty leader, wrote to Jackson:

The lowest classes of whites are now flogging the Cherokees with cowhides, hickories, and clubs. We are not safe in our homes....Send regular troops to protect us from these lawless assaults. If this is not done, we shall carry off nothing but the scars of the lash on our backs, and our oppressors will get all our money.[25]

The government was busy preparing for the mass migration. Former Georgia Governor Lumpkin, for years the Cherokees' most vocal foe, was named commissioner of the removal.

Jackson sent General John Ellis Wool and 7,000 troops to protect the Cherokee Nation from land invaders. Wool was as sympathetic to the Cherokees as Lumpkin was uncaring. He ordered the expulsion of all Georgia, Alabama, North Carolina, and Tennessee militia troops not under his command from the Cherokee country.

Lumpkin became irritated with Wool's insistence on fair treatment for the Indians. Wool soon tired of Lumpkin's criticism and asked to be relieved of his duty. He reported:

It is...vain to talk to people almost universally opposed to the treaty and who maintain that they never made such a treaty. So determined are they in their opposition that not one...however poor or destitute will receive either rations or clothing from the U.S. lest they compromise themselves in regard to the treaty. Many have said they will die before they leave this country.[26]

In January 1837, a group of Cherokees started West without government escort. They made the journey without major problems. These were the wealthy, aristocratic tribe members. Most of them had supported the treaty. This group of 600 took fancily clad horses, fat oxen, laughing children, slaves, and several wagons full of possessions. They traveled like the aristocrats they were, well dressed and well fed. The Ridge, who had

General John Ellis Wool was sent to protect Cherokees from forced removal, but quit when he saw that the government was determined to take their land at any cost.

received $24,000 for his Georgia property, had a coach for himself and his family, a carriage for his servants, and a wagon for his goods.

Two months later, another group left the eastern lands, following a different route. These 500 Cherokees were escorted by the government in a fleet of 11 flatboats. Their trip was plagued by disease—colds, influenza, measles, diarrhea, toothaches, injuries from accidents—and by alcohol. A third party of 365 left on an overland route in October. Fifteen died, 11 of them children.

Ross tried to reason with Martin Van Buren, who had won the presidential election. "We are not aware that the Senate could make valid that which was void," he said of the New Echota treaty.[27] Van Buren politely ignored Ross's plea. An 1838 memorial, a petition from the Cherokees that contained nearly 16,000 signatures, was returned marked "laid on table." The Senate refused even to discuss the matter.

The Cherokee chief told those tribesmen not already dispossessed to continue life as normal. They did. Spring of 1838 saw the sproutings of future crops on Cherokee farms.

Van Buren became infuriated with the Cherokees' stalling. He ordered Major General Winfield Scott to employ whatever force was needed to bring about Cherokee removal.

May 23, 1838—the day the Cherokees had to leave their old lands— saw the Indians tilling their fields. Their leader, John Ross, was in Washington, D.C. His people were neither physically nor emotionally ready for a long migration, Ross claimed.

Ross made one final plea to Van Buren. The U.S. President agreed to let the Cherokee president and his tribe stay on their land for two more years.

Georgia Governor George Gilmer, upon learning of Van Buren's shift of plans, became irate. He wrote Georgia Congressman William Dawson:

> If the United States troops shall attempt to resist our laws they will be required to leave the state….If the President refuses [to remove the Indians at once] the consequences must be upon his head.[28]

In other words, the Georgians meant to oust the Cherokees, even if it meant violence.

Van Buren learned of the threat and changed his mind. He ordered Scott, "Get the Indians out of Georgia, sir!"[29]

Chapter 9

Nunna dual Tsunyi—
"The Trail Where We Cried"

General Winfield Scott ordered the Cherokee roundup. The aging military man had fought in the Black Hawk War of 1832 and the Seminole Campaign of 1836. Like most Indian fighters, "Old Fuss and Feathers" had great respect for the tribes. But Scott was foremost a military man. When his commander-in-chief ordered him to move the Cherokees, he obeyed. Scott built more than two dozen forts and camps on Cherokee lands to hold the Cherokees until they could be moved West.

The Cherokees, herded like cattle, left behind the remnants of a proud and prosperous life. Their land now lay at the mercy of unscrupulous whites. Raiders at one farm could lead off dozens of healthy cattle. Others might find horses or wagons, saddles or rifles. Looters found harnesses, feather beds, blankets, chickens, knives and forks, pails, money, spinning wheels, salt, lumber, chains, baskets, ducks and geese, saws, shovels, potatoes, thread, pigs, beans, and weavers' tools.[1]

A Cherokee named Tsali became a martyr. A soldier prodded Tsali's wife with a bayonet for moving too slowly. Tsali stabbed the offender to death, then fled with his family into the North Carolina mountains. Other Cherokees who had escaped the soldiers' roundups protected him.

General Scott sent an army scout who knew Tsali to offer him a deal. If he and his sons pleaded guilty to murder, the soldiers would ignore

A political cartoon depicts the injustice of the treatment of the Cherokee Nation.

the rest of the Cherokees hidden in the North Carolina mountains. Tsali gave himself up. He and two sons were hanged, but a few hundred Cherokees were allowed to remain in North Carolina. Descendants of these mountain Cherokees still live in North Carolina, on what is now an Indian reservation.[2]

Scott told the incoming Cherokees they would be treated with kindness but would be hunted down if they tried to escape. The general said:

> My troops already occupy many positions in the country that you are to abandon, and thousands and thousands are approaching from every quarter to tender resistance and escape alike hopeless....Think

of this, my Cherokee brethren. I am an old warrior, and have been present at many a scene of slaughter; but spare me, I beseech you, the horror of witnessing the destruction of the Cherokees.[3]

At the same time, he told his troops:

The Cherokees, by the advances they have made in Christianity and civilization, are by far the most interesting tribe of Indians in the territorial limits of the United States....Simple indiscretions...may lead...to a general war and carnage—a result, in the case of these particular Indians, utterly abhorrent to the generous sympathies of the whole American people. Every possible kindness...must, therefore, be shown by the troops.[4]

Scott noted that "infants, superannuated persons, lunatics, and women in a helpless condition will all, in the removal, require particular attention."[5]

Troubles followed the Indians into the stockades. Many died because the U.S. government issued flour and other provisions that the Cherokees did not know how to prepare properly. Others died because of inadequate sanitation.

Rev. James Evans visited one of the stockades on June 16 and wrote:

The Cherokees are nearly all prisoners....The property of many has been taken and sold before their eyes for almost nothing....Many Cherokees who a few days ago were in comfortable circumstances are now victims of abject poverty....It is a work of war in a time of peace.[6]

The Cherokee Council, once a proud body governing a prosperous Nation, met in the stockade. Even though imprisoned, they still claimed their tribe's rule over Nation lands. They asked for a delay in the removal, so that older and weaker tribesmen would not be forced to march in the sweltering summer heat. Scott agreed to the request.

Some Cherokees decided to migrate West during the summer. One group of about 800 left June 6, 1838, on a route that took them along the Tennessee, Ohio, Mississippi, and Arkansas rivers. They boarded flatboats tied onto a steamer. One flatboat smashed up on rapids early in the trip. Hundreds escaped at the first opportunity.

A second group leaving the stockades soon afterward had terrible luck. Out of an estimated 875, some 300 became ill. By the time the group reached the western Cherokee lands, only 602 remained.

The worst drought in years dried the Upper Tennessee River. A third exile group had to take an overland route. They traveled north through Tennessee and Kentucky, then west through southern Illinois, Missouri, and Arkansas until they reached the land now known as Oklahoma. Of the original 1,070 Cherokees who made the journey, 700 ended up in the western territory. Most of the rest deserted along the way.

John Ross returned to his Cherokee homeland and found devastation. Only some stray pigs or cattle and a handful of white squatters inhabited the former Cherokee towns, which were now like ghost towns. He found the chiefs, Council members, and common people trapped in the stockades.

His fight to save the eastern Cherokee Nation was lost. Now he had a different mission. If Ross could not prevent the mass removal from taking place, at least he could make it as tolerable as possible. He agreed to take charge of the Cherokee removal.

Ross immediately produced results for his people. He arranged a daily allowance of 16 cents per day per person and 40 cents per horse. He demanded that liquor sales to the Cherokees cease. Thanks to Ross, General Scott did not cut down removal costs by eliminating soup, sugar, or coffee, all of which were considered useless luxuries by the War Department.[7]

On October 1, 1838, the 800-mile (1,288-kilometer) march westward began. Thirteen separate units of about 1,000 persons each gathered at Rattlesnake Springs, Tennessee, to depart. They brought 645 wagons and about 5,000 horses.

A sketch shows Cherokees dressed for the march to their new home.

The first group, led by Chief George Lowrey, formed a caravan a quarter-mile long. No formal ceremony marked the beginning of the march, but the group started with a prayer. In the middle of the prayer, a clap of thunder shook the party. William Shorey Coodey, one of the migrants, wrote:

The day was bright and beautiful, but a gloomy thoughtfulness was depicted in the lineaments of every face....A low sound of distant thunder fell on my ear—in an almost exact western direction a dark spiral cloud was rising above the horizon and sent forth a murmur I almost thought a voice of divine indignation for the wrong of my poor and unhappy countrymen.[8]

Then they started. An army private, John Burnett, recalled:

One can never forget the sadness and solemnity of that morning....When the bugle sounded and the wagons started rolling many of the children waved their little hands good-bye to their mountain homes.[9]

Three days after Lowrey's group left, a second group, headed by Elijah Hicks, departed. Jesse Bushyhead led a third group, and Evan Jones commanded a fourth. Every few days, through the rest of October and early November, different groups headed by tribal leaders left their departure point.

Illness set in almost immediately. Traveling parties had to stop so that doctors could tend to their patients. Sick people who had to be carried in wagons displaced animal fodder. The animals often ate poisonous plants along the trail and died. Cold weather accompanied the travelers much of the trip. Heavy rains made some roads impassable. Wagons collapsed; wagon wheels broke. An elderly chief named White Path fell to disease near Hopkinsville, Kentucky. His people buried him by the roadside, with a box painted to look like a marble tombstone and streamers around the box. It became a shrine for passing travelers.[10]

The Cherokees soon became disgusted with the government-supplied provisions. Rebecca Neugin, one of the migrants, recalled:

One of the most stirring images of the Trail of Tears is this painting by noted artist Robert Lindneux, who painted it many years after the actual march.

People got so tired of eating salt pork on the journey that my father would walk through the woods as we traveled, hunting for turkeys and deer, which he brought into the camp to feed us....When we stopped and prepared to cook our food, other emigrants who had been driven from our homes without opportunity to secure cooking utensils came to our camp to use our pots and kettles. There was much sickness among the emigrants and a great many little children died of whooping cough.[11]

The dead were left alongside the road or wherever travelers stopped. Today's campsite became tomorrow's cemetery. General Scott denied that there was excessive illness. "There is no more sickness among the Indians than might ordinarily take place amongst any other people under the same circumstances," he said. But a white observer watching the sad parade commented, "They are dying like flies."[12]

Another observer noted:

> The Indians as a whole carry on their countenance every thing but the appearance of happiness. Some carry a downcast digested look bordering on the

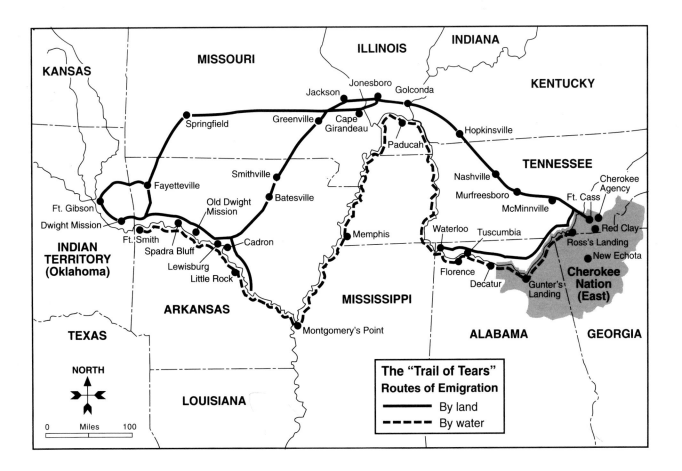

appearance of despair; others a wild frantic appearance as if to burst the chains of nature and pounce like a tiger upon their enemies.[13]

White civilians often traveled alongside the Cherokees. Some wanted to buy the Indians' remaining goods for a pittance. Others sold liquor. The Cherokees were exploited in other ways. Keepers of toll bridges raised their rates when the Cherokees came.

John Ross carefully packed the Nation's records and left with a later group. His wife, Quatie, became ill near Paducah, Kentucky. They abandoned the overland route and continued West by boat. Sleet, snow, and bitter winds accompanied them to a camp near Little Rock.

A child sick with pellagra cried for warmth. Quatie gave the child her blanket. The child recovered, but Quatie died that night.

Quatie Ross was one of many who perished. The last unit crawled into Oklahoma on March 24, 1839. The unit commanders gave a dreary census: Elijah Hicks' unit, 114 missing and 34 dead; Evan Jones' unit, 217 missing and 71 dead; Richard Drew's unit, 85 missing and 55 dead; and so on.[14]

Altogether, about 4,000 Cherokees out of 16,000 died on the forced march. A Georgia volunteer who later served in the Confederate Army wrote, "I fought through the Civil War and have seen men shot to pieces and slaughtered by the thousands, but the Cherokee removal was the cruelest work I ever saw."[15]

The Cherokees had a name for this removal—*Nunna dual Tsunyi*, "the trail where we cried."[16] Later, both whites and Cherokees would give it another name—"The Trail of Tears."

Chapter 10

"He Realized
His Fears"

Cherokee hatreds, animosities, and problems did not disappear when the Cherokees reached their new Oklahoma home. The pro-treaty faction and the antitreaty majority still disliked and distrusted each other. Now they had to contend with a third force: the Old Settlers, who had been there for a generation or more.

The recent arrivals who opposed the treaty greatly outnumbered the Old Settlers and the pro-treaty immigrants. They felt they should be the governing force. Their dislike and mistrust of the treaty faction traveled with them from the East to Oklahoma.

When some of Ross's followers saw John Ridge and Boudinot meeting with the western chiefs, they feared a deal that would deprive the antitreaty majority of tribal leadership. They decided to take action. Allen Ross distracted his father one night in June 1839, because John Ross would not have approved of what several hundred antitreaty Cherokees were plotting. The "blood law" would be invoked one more time. John Ridge, The Ridge, Elias Boudinot, and Stand Watie would die for selling Cherokee lands.

Would-be executioners drew lots for the "honor" of killing the traitors. Three men from each clan were summoned. Twelve men drew lots with the *X* mark. Four groups of three men went out after their victims.

The first band went to Honey Creek. The three masked men forced open John Ridge's cabin door, passed the rest of his family, and found their prey asleep in his bed. One aimed a pistol at him and pulled the trigger, but the weapon did not discharge. Then they dragged him from the bed and into his yard. The wiry Ridge put up a fight but was overpowered by his assailants. They slit his throat, stabbed him 25 times, and stomped on his body as his family watched helplessly.

A witness to the killing rode to Stand Watie's store and warned him of the death plan. Stand Watie escaped on a horse named Comet before the second group could reach him.

The Ridge was visiting a sick slave when three men neared. He left the cabin and walked down a path with a small boy. His attackers shot him 12 times. A courier sent to tell him of his son's death found The Ridge's lifeless body trampled by horses. The "blood law" that had once made him a hero now made him a victim.

A fourth group went to the house Boudinot was building. The three men told him their families were sick and needed medical supplies. Since Boudinot was in charge of "public medicines," he suspected nothing. When he turned, one man stabbed him in the back. As he screamed and fell, another split his head open with a tomahawk.

Rev. Worcester saw Boudinot's attackers fleeing the scene. Even though he opposed the treaty Boudinot had signed, Worcester later wrote that Boudinot "had fallen a victim…to his honest zeal for the preservation of his people. In his own view, he risked his life to save his people from ruin, and he realized his fears."[1]

The killings of the Ridges and Boudinot might have satisfied some feelings for revenge, but otherwise they solved nothing. Killing led to killing. For years, blood flowed in a continuous murder spree.[2]

Nonetheless, the pro-treaty, antitreaty, and Old Settler factions were able to cooperate in forming a new government. They created a new capital in the town of Tahlequah, united eastern and western land claims under one government, created a new constitution, and held elections in September 1839. Ross won the September election. A westerner, David Vann, was chosen vice-president. Still, differences among the three groups lingered for years. Only in 1846, when President James K. Polk called all three sides to Washington, did they sign a treaty ending the Nation's internal hostilities.

Forced to live on reservations, many Cherokees became depressed by the lack of freedom and loss of their traditional way of life.

The 1846 treaty led to relative peace in the Nation until the Civil War. When shots were fired upon Fort Sumter, South Carolina, in 1861, factions reemerged. Pro-treaty Cherokees, many of whom owned slaves, favored the Confederacy. Most of the Nation preferred the northern Union but advocated neutrality.

Early Confederate victories persuaded most Cherokees to side with the South. Stand Watie, through his military skill, rose to the rank of general in the Confederate Army. Ross, against his better judgment, signed a treaty with the South in late 1861. The following year, the war turned in favor of the North.

Ross, while visiting Washington, D.C., in 1862, was arrested for treason. President Abraham Lincoln soon pardoned him. Lincoln was lenient to the Cherokees, but after his assassination in 1865, the U.S. government demanded concessions from the Nation. The Cherokees' greatest hero, John Ross, died a year later while negotiating a new treaty, which was adopted soon after his death.

The treaty preserved the Cherokee Nation but freed the Cherokees' slaves. The Cherokees had to yield land. More important, they were forced to allow a railroad to run through their Nation.

This treaty spelled the beginning of the end for the Cherokees. Now they would have no control over who passed through their lands. Texas cattlemen and eastern farmers now could admire—and covet—the Cherokee holdings. An 1898 agreement with the federal government led to the Nation's demise. Lands reverted from tribal to individual ownership. This meant that individual Cherokees could sell land without tribal approval to white settlers or the U.S. government. The Nation could be peacefully diminished, bit by bit.

By the end of the 19th century, the Nation was doomed. Oklahoma territory applied for statehood. The Cherokees asked that the new state be named Sequoyah, after the man who created their alphabet. Congress stuck with the name Oklahoma.

On November 16, 1907, Oklahoma became the 46th state of the Union, and the autonomous Cherokee Nation, land which had been promised "forever" by so many treaties, was no more.

Formal dissolution of the Cherokee Nation did not mean the end of the Cherokees as a people. More than 50,000 descendants of the Nation now live throughout the United States, making the Cherokees the largest Native American group in the country. Over the years, Cherokees frequently married outsiders, and most persons with Cherokee blood are a result of these mixed marriages, including Oklahoma's most famous citizen, cowboy humorist Will Rogers.

Most Cherokees live in eastern Oklahoma, where their ancestors moved in the early 1800s. More than 16,000 acres of Oklahoma land was reorganized in 1934 under Cherokee trusteeship.

Six thousand Cherokees live in western North Carolina. These are the descendants of the tribesmen saved by Tsali's sacrifice. Native American actors in the town of Cherokee annually re-create the Tsali story in a play titled *Unto These Hills*.

In their way, the North Carolina residents keep alive the message of the last Cherokee memorial to the United States:

> The title of the Cherokee people to their lands is the most ancient, pure, and absolute known to man; its date is beyond human record....The Cherokee people have existed as a distinct community...for a period extending into the antiquity beyond the dates and records and memory of man....These attributes have never been relinquished by the Cherokee people...and cannot...be dissolved by the expulsion of the Nation from its own territory.[3]

An artist's depiction of an Indian family leaving their home to begin the Trail of Tears.

NOTES

Chapter 1

1. Gloria Jahoda, *The Trail of Tears: The Story of the American Indian Removals 1813–1855* (New York: Holt, Reinhart and Winston, 1975), p. 230.
2. Ibid., p. 231.
3. Rebecca Neugin, *Memories of the Trail,* quoted in Richard Thornton, *American Indian Holocaust and Survival* (Norman, Okla.: University of Oklahoma Press, 1987), p. 117.

Chapter 2

1. Grace Steele Woodward, *The Cherokees* (Norman, Okla.: University of Oklahoma Press, 1987), p. 18.
2. Ibid., p. 33.
3. Samuel Carter III, *Cherokee Sunset: A Nation Betrayed* (Garden City, New York: Doubleday, 1976), p. 18.
4. Woodward, p. 51.
5. Dale Van Every, *Disinherited: The Lost Birthright of the American Indian* (New York: William Morrow, 1966), p. 3.
6. Carter, p. 7.
7. Ronald Wright, *Stolen Continents: The Americans through Indian Eyes since 1492* (Boston: Houghton-Mifflin, 1992), p. 97.
8. Carter, p. 8.
9. Wright, p. 109.
10. Carter, p. 9.
11. Wright, p. 113.

Chapter 3

1. Van Every, p. 89.
2. Herman J. Viola, *After Columbus: The Smithsonian Chronicle of the American Indian* (Washington, D.C.: Smithsonian Books, 1990), p. 131.
3. Carter, p. 32.
4. Ibid., p. 5.
5. Woodward, p. 135.
6. Carter, p. 36.
7. Wright, p. 219.

Chapter 4

1. Carter, p. 23.
2. Van Every, p. 59.
3. Ibid., p. 50.
4. Carter, p. 49.
5. Van Every, p. 49.
6. Carter, p. 64.
7. Ibid., p. 68.
8. Ibid., p. 76.

Chapter 5

1. Van Every, p. 99.
2. Carter, p. 57.
3. Van Every, p. 99.
4. Carter, p. 57.
5. Jahoda, p. 36.
6. Woodward, p. 148.
7. Carter, p. 73.
8. Van Every, p. 103.
9. Jahoda, p. 39.
10. Francis Paul Prucha, ed., *Cherokee Removal: The "William Penn" Essays and Other Writings* (Knoxville: University of Tennessee Press, 1981), p. 168.

11. Woodward, p. 136.
12. Wright, p. 214.
13. Ibid.
14. Van Every, p. 114.
15. Ibid., p. 117.
16. Carter, p. 101.
17. Ibid., p. 135.

Chapter 6
1. Van Every, p. 32.
2. Jahoda, p. 26.
3. John Ehle, *Trail of Tears* (New York: Anchor Doubleday, 1988), p. 26.

Chapter 7
1. Carter, p. 90.
2. Woodward, p. 162.
3. Carter, p. 106.
4. Van Every, p. 156.
5. Carter, p. 107.
6. Van Every, p. 145.
7. Carter, p. 131.
8. Van Every, p. 147.

Chapter 8
1. Van Every, p. 147.
2. Carter, p. 135.
3. Ibid., p. 136.
4. Van Every, p. 63.
5. Carter, p. 140.
6. Ibid., p. 144.
7. Ibid., p. 142.
8. Ibid., p. 147.
9. Van Every, p. 196.
10. Carter, p. 161.
11. Woodward, p. 182.
12. Carter, p. 165.
13. Ibid., p. 170.
14. Ibid., p. 182.
15. Jahoda, p. 221.
16. Woodward, p. 186.
17. Van Every, p. 204.

18. Woodward, p. 187.
19. Carter, p. 185.
20. Ibid., p. 186.
21. Ibid., p. 188.
22. Woodward, p. 193.
23. Carter, p. 191.
24. Woodward, p. 221.
25. Van Every, p. 224.
26. Woodward, p. 194.
27. Carter, p. 208.
28. Ibid., p. 228.
29. Jahoda, p. 228.

Chapter 9
1. Jahoda, p. 232.
2. Ibid., p. 227.
3. Van Every, p. 240.
4. Woodward, p. 204.
5. Jahoda, p. 230.
6. Ibid., p. 232.
7. Carter, p. 16.
8. Jahoda, p. 233.
9. Woodward, p. 215.
10. Van Every, p. 247.
11. Neugin, p. 117.
12. Jahoda, p. 231.
13. Van Every, p. 249.
14. Carter, p. 264.
15. Richard Thornton, *American Indian Holocaust and Survival* (Norman, Okla.: University of Oklahoma Press, 1987), p. 116.
16. Ibid., p. 114.

Chapter 10
1. Carter, p. 270.
2. Jahoda, p. 241.
3. Van Every, p. 15.

FOR FURTHER READING

Carter, Samuel III. *Cherokee Sunset: A Nation Betrayed.* Garden City, New York: Doubleday, 1976.

Ehle, John. *Trail of Tears.* New York: Anchor Doubleday, 1988.

Everett, Dianna. *The Texas Cherokees: A People between Two Fires 1819–1840.* Norman, Okla.: University of Oklahoma Press, 1990.

Foreman, Grant. *Indian Removal: The Emigration of the Five Civilized Tribes.* Norman, Okla.: University of Oklahoma Press, 1972.

Jahoda, Gloria. *The Trail of Tears: The Story of the American Indian Removals 1813–1855.* New York: Holt, Reinhart and Winston, 1975.

Prucha, Francis Paul, ed. *Cherokee Removal: The "William Penn" Essays and Other Writings.* Knoxville: University of Tennessee Press, 1981.

Thornton, Richard. *American Indian Holocaust and Survival.* Norman, Okla.: University of Oklahoma Press, 1987.

Van Every, Dale. *Disinherited: The Lost Birthright of the American Indian.* New York: William Morrow, 1966.

Viola, Herman J. *After Columbus: The Smithsonian Chronicle of the American Indian.* Washington, D.C.: Smithsonian Books, 1990.

Woodward, Grace Steele. *The Cherokees.* Norman, Okla.: University of Oklahoma Press, 1987.

Wright, Ronald. *Stolen Continents: The Americans through Indian Eyes since 1492.* Boston: Houghton-Mifflin, 1992.

Zinn, Howard. *A People's History of the United States.* New York: Harper Perennial, 1990.

INDEX